TRANSFORMATIONS, STYLE,
and MEANING

XEROX COLLEGE PUBLISHING

Waltham, Massachusetts / Toronto

Transformations, Style, and Meaning

RODERICK A. JACOBS
University of California, San Diego

PETER S. ROSENBAUM
Teachers College, Columbia University

Preface

Our courses with their tear-out workbooks and four-pound anthologies are elaborate evasions of the real problem. They permit us to put in our time and do almost anything else we'd rather be doing instead of buckling down to the hard work of making a difference in the student's understanding and manipulation of language.

F. Christensen   (1963)

This book, designed for students of language and style, has three primary objectives. The first is to show that although the relation of form to meaning is not a direct one, it is indeed a very systematic one. The second is to describe and explain major aspects of English sentence structure within the framework of the important theory of language developed in recent years by generative-transformational grammarians. The third is to make the student aware of the semantic and stylistic consequences of choosing one syntactic form over another.

Such an awareness, of course, does not automatically lead to good writing or sensitive reading on the part of the student. Too many other factors — imagination, sensibility, logic, a feeling for words — are involved. But both from the point of view of the student writer and the student reader, a sound linguistic description can be very useful. It should provide an insightful way to expand the syntactic inventory that he actually draws from in writing, it should sensitize him to significant stylistic differences between apparent paraphrases, and perhaps it should remind him of possibilities unexploited as he looks over a first draft of his own.

But first, a note on transformational grammar and its background. Creativity in language is not the monopoly of novelists, poets, and playwrights. Every normal human being has the capacity to create and understand sentences he has never heard before. The child hears a fairly small set of utterances and then begins not just to replicate them but to construct new sentences, some of which he recognizes

v

as unacceptable from their effect on the hearer. These he may reconstruct in order to be understood. In essence the child is creating and revising a theory as to how a particular language works. The ease with which this is achieved and its relative independence of intelligence suggest that this linguistic theory-construction ability is inborn.

Such a theory of one's native language may be labeled as a *grammar*. This grammar consists of a set of rules which the child cannot state explicitly although they obviously govern the sentences he produces.

Following the earliest work of Chomsky, transformational linguists have regarded language as rule-governed behavior. They seek to make explicit those rules we intuitively follow — and those that skilled users such as Faulkner, Shakespeare, or John Kenneth Galbraith intuitively follow.

Such an approach to language is far from novel. It can be traced back at least to the universal grammars of the seventeenth and eighteenth centuries. The authors of the famous *Grammaire Générale et Raisonnée* (1660) tried not merely to list and classify the data of French and Latin but to offer an explanation of such data and to show how languages exploit universal processes of logic.

By the end of the nineteenth century this great tradition of universal grammar was dead. The universal grammarians had lacked the precise tools to formulate rules capable of accounting for the complex formal interrelationships of the sentences of any natural language. Moreover, the remarkable successes in the last century of Rask, Grimm, and the other comparative grammarians in tracing very precisely the interrelationships and historical development of the Indo-European languages had exposed the imprecisions and theoretical confusions of the universal grammarians. The tradition continued in a somewhat less ambitious but more systematic form in the very useful traditional scholarly grammars of Sweet, Curme, Jespersen, Poutsma, Kruizinga, and a number of other European linguists. Jespersen's seven-volume grammar of English, the most thorough and insightful one yet produced, is a laborious listing with all kinds of facts, suppositions, and guesses intermixed.

The newer structural linguists — Bloomfield, Bloch, Fries, Zellig Harris — sought to make linguistics a respectable "science" by developing a scientific method ignoring intuitive knowledge, which was not verifiable, and concentrating on those aspects of language accessible to all, starting with the phonetic level, formulating a "phonological" level presenting only the linguistically-significant contrasts among sounds, and eventually working up to a semantic level, though this was never attained — in fact even the level of syntax is only very superficially described. Basically such grammars were often primarily methodological texts on how to formulate categories and arrange data. The surviving heirs of this tradition — tagmemics and stratificational grammar — still reflect this preoccupation with data processing, although they have inevitably been influenced by transformational work. In fact, in some areas the rather confused tagmemic theory has anticipated more recent transformational insights.

The publication of Chomsky's pioneer monograph *Syntactic Structures* (1957) heralded an amazingly rapid revolution in the field of linguistics. Instead of producing still more technique for segmenting utterances and classifying the segments, Chomsky returned to the older tradition of seeking to account for the native speaker's linguistic intuitions and creativity. He sought to do this with grammars which were not carefully tabulated lists of data but sets of rules which, if followed, would produce (he borrowed from symbolic logic the term *generate*) the sentences of a language and account for the interrelationships perceived by the native speaker although not manifest in the actual linguistic forms produced. He developed the formal rules from recent mathematical work in set theory and recursiveness. Here was a way to express the insights of the old universal grammarians, a way closed to them because they had lacked the theoretical tools. Chomsky succeeded in showing that earlier structuralist grammars of human languages were fundamentally incapable of dealing with some of the most important properties of language. The sets of rules used could not account for the infinite set of sentences that makes up any human language. The empirical claims made by such grammars were limited by their format: listing of categories and items, procedures for cutting up sentences, and so forth. Consequently such grammars could do little to help us understand the nature of a language system which could be learned so rapidly by small children, a system allowing infinite creativity to its users. The grammars, or rather fragments — since no one has yet written a full one — could not explain how native speakers understand expressions in one way rather than another or how they were able to make use of certain kinds of syntactic information not obviously present on the surface of sentences to interpret them correctly. Chomsky's vastly more powerful model of language included two principal levels of structure: a deep structure which, in some not always precise manner, embodied the meaning, and a surface structure which was the set of forms which are converted into sound or writing as the sentences of a language. The deep structure was a level produced (or generated) by a set of rules, called *Phrase Structure Rules,* enumerating the basic parts of a sentence, e.g.,

Sentence → Noun Phrase   Auxiliary   Verb Phrase

or

S → NP   AUX   VP

Then a set of transformations, some obligatory, some optional, converted these deep structures into surface structures. Certain very simple sentences to which only obligatory transformations had been applied were called *kernel sentences.* The transformations were not rules like the one illustrated above. Instead of expanding elements such as sentence, noun phrase, auxiliary, verb phrase into their component parts, transformations changed the structure of entire sentence units, deleting, substituting, and adjoining forms in a sentence structure. Earlier structural grammars had almost inevitably confined themselves to the less powerful phrase structure rules. Chomsky showed that only by using both kinds of rules could a grammar come close to making explicit what it is a native speaker knows about his native language.

One rather disarming characteristic of Chomsky's insistence on explicitness was that the principles and claims underlying his theory of language were clear and therefore open to challenge. These claims could be disproven by empirical investigation not only of many languages but also of psychology and neurology. *Syntactic Structures* set off explorations by generations of doctoral students and their professors of scores and scores of languages, of language acquisition by children, and especially of the English language, mother tongue of most of the investigators.

As a consequence much of the complex machinery popularly associated with transformational grammar has been scrapped. Even the initially indispensable desire for explicit precision that Chomsky inherited from structuralism has waned as the importance of expressing semantic insights has come to overshadow the criterion of expressibility within a formalizable rule. Far from separating syntax and semantics, as Chomsky did so brilliantly in 1957, many transformational grammarians today are inclined to treat them as inseparable. New transformational grammars are being written which are semantically based. This book inevitably draws upon such attempts, though linguistic theory of this kind is very much in a state of flux and likely to remain so for years. Yet most of the basic insights discovered or rediscovered by Chomsky have been found both valid and productive. We hope that this book will acquaint you with some of the most interesting among them and convey some of the excitement that the exploration of human language can engender.

We wish to express an especial debt to our teacher of linguistics, Noam Chomsky, to Edward Klima for his work in both English syntax and literary analysis, and to the critic and teacher F. R. Leavis, who showed us that true paraphrase is impossible.

Contents

TRANSFORMATIONS, STYLE,
and MEANING

Form and Meaning in Language

1

Language most shewes a man: speake that I may see
thee. It springs out of the most retired and inmost parts
of us, and is the Image of the Parent of it, the mind.

Ben Jonson (1572–1637)

In an important sense speech is just sounds, puffs of noisy air set
in vibration by the vocal bands, not so different acoustically from
the hiss of a steam engine, the clatter of a typewriter, or the wail
of a baby. But if there really were no difference, you would not
be sitting here reading this book.

Certain sounds arranged in particular ways become words, and
words arranged in particular ways become sentences. The form these
sentences take determines their meaning. Or alternatively it could
be argued that some aspect of the meaning of these sentences
determines their form. In any event the speaker of a language
intuitively associates meanings with particular language forms. No
one knows the exact nature of the relationship between form and
meaning. One of the major goals of linguistics, perhaps *the* major
one, is to make this relationship explicit. Since the native speaker
is continually exploiting this relationship, the linguist seeks to dis-
cover what a speaker knows, without realizing it, that enables him
to produce and understand the sentences of his language. What are
the language abilities of the speaker of a human language? Some
of the answers can be discovered by examining carefully the language
he speaks. What relevant properties distinguish language?

All human languages share certain properties, not all of them
obvious. For example, *synonymy*, the basic identity of meaning
between two or more utterances, is to be found in every language.
For example, in languages using both active and passive con-

structions, for almost every passive sentence there is an active one with the same basic meaning. No definition of meaning can be given here for there is no satisfactory one. In this book two types of meaning are discussed: *basic meaning* and *surface meaning*. Together they constitute the most central part of what we call meaning in language. *Basic meaning* is roughly what two (or more) paraphrases of a sentence have in common. In both the following sentences:

(1) It would be picked over at night by the rats with their twitching snouts.

(2) At night the rats would pick it over with their twitching snouts.

Maureen Duffy, *The Paradox Players*

the same creatures are doing something. They are doing the same things at the same time. In other words the same truth conditions prevail. What is true for one sentence is true for the other. Most people would say the sentences have the same meaning. Basically this claim is correct.

But at another level no two distinct sentences can be paraphrases of each other. A part of the full meaning of any sentence is communicated by the form chosen for the sentence. As the old maxim goes, "It's not just *what* you say; it's *how* you say it." If the basic meaning of a sentence is equivalent in a very loose sense to "what you say," "how you say it" provides what we shall refer to as the *surface meaning*, the extra dimension of meaning communicated by the *style* of the writer. The skilled writer is aware, often without fully realizing it, of a number of alternative ways to express a basic meaning. This is best explained by another illustration.

When George Eliot was working on the manuscript of her novel *Middlemarch*, she first wrote this sentence about a Captain Lydgate:

(3) He had never thought what it would be to borrow.

But then she revised it to read this way:

(4) He had never thought what borrowing would be to him.

George Eliot made a choice between two basically synonymous strings of words. But to George Eliot they cannot have been fully synonymous. Perhaps she felt that the *borrowing* idea should not appear at the end, where it seems to dominate the sentence. Phrased the original way, the sentence almost demands a hesitation, a pause, before *to borrow*, as if borrowing were an unspeakable activity.

Presumably the author did not want this degree of prominence for the *borrowing* idea. Instead the important end position is given to *him*. The grammatical subject *borrowing* is still important as the subject of the sentence.[1] The result is that emphasis has been placed on the incongruity, from Captain Lydgate's point of view, of *his* being in a situation where borrowing might be necessary. Lydgate's horror culminates with the final *him*. The world of borrowing, previously a despised, alien one, has now taken over even *him!* So two sentences with the same basic meaning have as a result of their differing forms additional meaning. Style, the use of one form rather than another, may provide an important kind of meaning. Since this results from the surface form of a sentence, it is called here *surface meaning*. The distinction between *basic meaning* and *surface meaning* is in some ways, an artificial one but is very useful for discussing writing. We shall be concerned now with *basic* meaning.

One basic meaning may be expressed in a number of different forms. But also one form may stand for more than one basic meaning. All languages have sentences which have more than one meaning. Ambiguity is a universal property of language. Ambiguity, schematically described here,

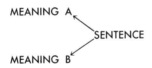

and synonymy,

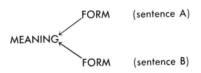

[1] In fact the use of the *-ing* form *borrowing* rather than the infinitive to *borrow* is quite significant. The infinitive suggests less reality than the more active sounding *-ing* form. To take a clearer example, the sentence

Soames did not like to give in

makes no assumption that Soames did in fact give in. But

Soames did not like giving in

more easily suggests that Soames had really given in, though he had not liked it.

are two universal characteristics of language that show meaning to be related to form in an indirect way. The grammar of every language must embody such characteristics. A grammar can be defined as the set of principles to which every native speaker unconsciously adheres whenever he produces or understands sentences of his language.

Take the sentence:

(5) A man can be destroyed but not defeated.

Hemingway, *The Old Man and the Sea*

Hemingway's sentence is an affirmation containing two basic statements about man, joined by the conjunction *but:*

(6) A man can be destroyed.
(7) Not defeated.

But statement number two, in isolation, isn't very coherent. But when you read the full sentence you know, without really knowing *why,* that it must mean

(8) A man cannot be defeated.

In fact Hemingway could have written the sentence like this:

(9) A man can be destroyed but a man cannot be defeated.

Any normal speaker of English understands this last sentence in the same way as Hemingway's original one, despite the difference in form. What does the speaker know which allows him to make such a judgment? One possible answer to this question should appear when the sentences are lined up:

(9) A man can be destroyed but a man cannot be defeated.
(5) A man can be destroyed but   not   defeated.

The words missing from Hemingway's version all occur earlier in the sentence. Thus the second mention of *a man* has been deleted, so has the second mention of *can* and that of *be.* It seems that individual words or groups of words can be deleted from a sentence without affecting meaning. The condition is usually that the deleted words must be present elsewhere in the sentence. These processes of changing form without changing basic meaning are called *transformations.*

Exercises for Chapter One

1. Some of the sentences below are basically ambiguous; others are not. Show the different basic meanings of the ambiguous one by writing unambiguous paraphrases for each meaning:
   (a) Pam enjoyed boring old ladies.
   (b) I will take this up with my mother.
   (c) The chicken was ready to eat.
   (d) Go home or I'll report you.
   (e) Juan liked Pepsi and Maria Coca-Cola.

2. What meaning differences can you observe between the following?
   (a) The men cursed. The women nagged. The children continually snivelled. All this drove him to leave the town and find work somewhere else.
   (b) The cursing of the men, the nagging of the women, and the continual snivelling of the children all drove him to leave the town and find work somewhere else.

3. Comment on the use of the word *grammar* in the following sentence:

   This grammar, published in 1968, attempted to make explicit the internal grammar of a native speaker of modern Flemish.

BIBLIOGRAPHY

CHOMSKY, NOAM. *Language and Mind.* New York: Harcourt, 1968, Chapter 2.
OHMANN, RICHARD. "Generative Grammars and the Concept of Literary Style" in M. Steinmann, *New Rhetorics.* New York: Scribner, 1967.

Deep Structure and Surface Structure

2

The general assumption of [seventeenth and eighteenth century] Cartesian linguistics is that the surface organization of a sentence may not give a true and full representation of the grammatical relations that play a role in determining its semantic content.

Noam Chomsky (1966)

The sentence following sounds quite awkward:

(1) *It pained him* that he did not know well what politics meant and *it pained him* that he did not know where the universe ended.

This rather strange sentence is actually a paraphrase of one written by James Joyce. But in his version Joyce omitted the second mention of

it pained him

and wrote

(2) It pained him that he did not know well what politics meant and that he did not know where the universe ended.

James Joyce, *A Portrait of the Artist as a Young Man*

He might also have chosen to delete the second occurrence of *that* but this is less important. An important word in this sentence is *well*. Without it, the subject and verb going with "what politics meant" would have been identical with those going with "where the universe ended," that is,

he did not know.

Joyce's sentence could then have been paraphrased

(3)   It pained him that he did not know what politics meant and where the universe ended.

But *well* differentiates the extent of knowledge about politics from that about the universe. To a sensitive reader it might suggest that Joyce's young Stephen Daedalus did, perhaps with immature pride, believe he knew *something* about the meaning of politics, though not about where the universe ended. The presence of *well* also enables Joyce to avoid deleting the second "he did not know," especially if he wants to stress the boy's awareness of his ignorance. The kind of meaning involved here is the subtler surface meaning treated in stylistic rather than grammatical analysis. As we suggested earlier, the notions of *basic* and *surface* meanings are useful though sometimes artificial. Here the two merge.

It should now be apparent that the speaker's ability to understand certain sentences as synonymous cannot be a result of his having memorized all the synonymous sentences beforehand. Every day he comes across new sentences, some of which may be synonymous. The speaker knows that certain kinds of sentences are transformed variants of other sentences. You may never have heard the sentence

(4)   It is easy to feed the chickens on Mondays.

but you recognize it as basically synonymous with the following sentence:

(5)   The chickens are easy to feed on Mondays.

As you have seen, one important type of transformation involves deletion under identity. You may account for the synonymy of two sentences by showing that elements of a sentence had been deleted because they were present elsewhere in the sentence. But other kinds of deletion are possible. These also preserve meaning but they do not require deleted elements to be identical to others in the sentence. Look again at Hemingway's sentence from Chapter One:

A man can be destroyed but not defeated.

Two possible actions are stated: *destroying* and *defeating*. But in neither case is *a man* to carry out the action. Semantically, *a man* has these actions done to him by someone or something else. Semantically *a man* is the receiver, the object of *destroyed* and *defeated.* Who or what then is the *actor?* In other words, what is the semantic subject? Read the sentence again and you should see that the doer of the action must be some indefinite entity, *someone* or *something* rather than, say, *a fisherman* or *a shark.* Indeed, Hemingway's sentence can be revised to include such an indefinite element.

(6) A man can be destroyed by $\begin{Bmatrix} \text{someone} \\ \text{something} \end{Bmatrix}$ but not defeated by $\begin{Bmatrix} \text{someone} \\ \text{something} \end{Bmatrix}$.

The actors are represented by the indefinite element *someone* or *something.* They can be deleted from a sentence without affecting the basic meaning. When sentences such as Hemingway's are interpreted by a speaker of English, he understands more than is actually contained in the form of the sentence. It is as if the sentence had an underlying structure actually containing the *someone* or *something*, a structure altered in form but not meaning by a process deleting the indefinite actor or agent.

It is indeed quite reasonable to describe sentences as having two crucial levels of structure. One level, the deep structure, is quite abstract, representing the basic *meaning* of the sentence. The other level, the surface structure, gives the actual *form* of a sentence as it is spoken or written. The speaker or hearer reconstructs the implicit meaning or deep structure of a sentence from the surface structure. The transformational rule relating these two structures deletes the phrase *by someone* to get to the surface structure.[1]

Is there really any evidence for deleting indefinite elements? Or is the rule just an invention to account for something missing in Hemingway's sentence? Are such rules present elsewhere in English? Or are indefinite elements omissible only when *by* occurs before them in passive sentences:

(7) He was shot by someone.
(8) He was shot.

In fact the rule does indeed appear elsewhere in English. Note the logical identity of meaning in the following pairs of sentences:

---

[1] For practical reasons we talk of deleting words or phrases rather than deleting the more abstract deep structure elements corresponding to such words or phrases.

(9) It was easy for *someone* to please Ernest.
(10) It was easy to please Ernest.
(11) The path was hard for *anyone* to find.
(12) The path was hard to find.

In most cases the indefinite elements may be deleted.

The ability to fill in mentally elements of a sentence which have been deleted because of identity with other elements which are present accounts for your understanding of one kind of synonymy. The ability to fill in mentally the indefinite elements which have been deleted accounts for your understanding of another kind of synonymy. What about that other universal characteristic of language, *ambiguity*. Take the sentences:

(13) Mrs. Skolnik fed her dog biscuits.
(14) The police were ordered to stop rioting on campus.

The first sentence means either

(15) Mrs. Skolnik fed biscuits to her dog.

or

(16) Mrs. Skolnik fed dog biscuits to her.

There are, of course, other ambiguities but these are the important interpretations for present purposes. Sentences (15) and (16) are distinct and unambiguous. Sentence (15) is subject to a transformation, called the indirect object transformation, which first shifts the phrase *to her dog* to the position before the previous noun phrase

(17) Mrs. Skolnik fed to her dog biscuits.

and then deletes the preposition *to:*

(18) Mrs. Skolnik fed her dog biscuits.

which is the same as sentence (13). Interestingly, the fact that *her dog* is in a different phrase from *biscuits* may be marked by a slight pause between them when the sentence is spoken and also by special stress on the words.

But the sentence standing for the other interpretation:

(16) Mrs. Skolnik fed dog biscuits to her.

is also subject to the same transformation. This time it shifts *to her* in front of the previous noun phrase, which happens to be *dog biscuits:*

(17)   Mrs. Skolnik fed to her dog biscuits.

Then again the *to* is deleted:

(19)   Mrs. Skolnik fed her dog biscuits.

which is again sentence (13). Sentence (16), which is quite distinct from (15), has been transformed into a sentence with the same sequence of words as the sentence resulting from the transformation of (15). So sentence (13) has two distinct deep structures and therefore two different meanings.

Sentence (14)

(14)   The police were ordered to stop rioting on campus.

is multiply ambiguous. One of the two most obvious interpretations:

(20)   The police were ordered to stop *anyone* from rioting on campus.

The indefinite element *anyone* may be deleted from (20). The result of this transformation is sentence (14), with the meaning (20). But sentence (14) also has this meaning:

(21)   The police were ordered for *the police* to stop rioting on campus.

The transformation removing identical elements deletes the second mention of *the police*. The *for* is, in modern English, deleted, and the result is sentence (14) with the meaning (21). Since (14) has two distinct deep structures it has two distinct meanings. The grammar thus provides a principled basis for the speaker's understanding of the ambiguity. The grammar relates form and meaning by postulating transformational processes converting deep structure, representing *meaning*, into surface structure, representing *form*. This grammatical framework provides an explanation for your ability as a speaker of English to detect:

1. synonymy resulting from identity deletion.
2. synonymy resulting from deletion of indefinite elements.
3. ambiguity.

None of these abilities could have resulted from rote memorization of all synonymous and ambiguous sentences. In fact they reveal an even more impressive ability. Knowing English means knowing how to produce and understand an infinite number of English sentences you have never encountered before. It is quite unlikely, for example, that you have ever encountered any of the sentences in this chapter before; still, you have probably understood and accepted all of them as sentences of English. In other words, when you learned a language you did not learn the sentences of the language one at a time. Even if you and some language teacher were to live more years than the number of seconds in the estimated lifetime of the universe, the language teacher could not recite to you all of the sentences of English numbering twenty words or less. And this assumes that you stop neither for sleeping nor eating.

The meaning of all this has to do with the nature of linguistic knowledge. Not only, apparently, does the speaker of a language know the deep and surface structures of his language; he has also acquired some finite procedure allowing him (1) to produce brand new sentence structures most commonly never before uttered in the history of the language, and (2) to comprehend novel sentences.

This is a generative ability involving the production of an infinite number of objects, sentences, using a finite brain and finite knowledge. And this generative ability is very precise. For instance every normal speaker of English knows that sentence (22) is a fully grammatical sentence in English whereas sentence (23) is not a sentence of English at all.

(22)   His stomach was like a watermelon underneath his vest and there were rolls of fat on the back of his neck.

Carson McCullers, *The Member of the Wedding*

(23)   * Of on vest neck his rolls were of fat like a watermelon was his there and a.

Thus, two more items can be added to the inventory of skills possessed by the speaker

4. generative ability
5. recognition of ungrammaticality

These abilities are characteristic of the speakers of all human languages.

In recent years a theory of language and linguistic structure has been evolved which provides a perspective in which to see how these abilities arise and how they are related. The following chapters develop some of the more interesting and important aspects of this theory.

Exercises for Chapter Two

1. Here are some more sentences, some of which may be ambiguous. For the ambiguous sentences differentiate their various meanings by writing unambiguous paraphrases for each meaning:
   (a) Visiting relatives can be a bore.
   (b) He took sadistic delight in taunting young boys and girls.
   (c) James washed the dishes slowly and carefully.
   (d) After the snowstorm, the city was almost completely paralyzed.
   (e) My great aunt dislikes smoking cigarettes.
   (f) The old recluse doesn't beat his wife because he likes her.
2. The following sentences illustrate the phenomenon of transformational deletion. In each case, rewrite the sentence reconstructing the deleted materials.
   (a) I can't find my car nor my friend, Sam, his motorcycle.
   (b) My English instructor thought my poem was the best he had ever seen.
   (c) It strikes the prosecution as strange that the janitor failed to see the crime and to report it.
3. Why would a grammar dealing only with surface structures be inadequate as a model of what a native speaker knows?

BIBLIOGRAPHY

CHOMSKY, NOAM. *Language and Mind.* New York: Harcourt, 1968, Chapter 1.

JACOBS, RODERICK A. and PETER S. ROSENBAUM. *An Introduction to Transformational Grammar: Grammars 1 and 2.* Waltham, Mass.: Ginn, 1970.

POSTAL, PAUL M. "Underlying and Superficial Linguistic Structure" in J. Emig, J.T. Fleming, and H.M. Popp (eds.), *Language and Learning.* New York: Harcourt, 1966.

Constituents and the Transformation Process

3

You are about to enter upon one of the most useful, and, when rightly pursued, one of the most interesting studies in the whole circle of science. If, however, you, like many a misguided youth, are under the impression that the study of grammar is dry and irksome, and a matter of little consequence, I trust I shall succeed in removing from your mind, all such false notions and ungrounded prejudices.

Samuel Kirkham (1826)

The various native abilities exhibited by speakers of natural languages suggest that sentences have two main levels of structure, a deep structure and a surface structure. The former represents the meaning of the sentence, the latter the form of the sentence. But what exactly are sentence structures?

In the same way that an army is the sum of its divisions, and a division the sum of its battalions, a sentence is the sum of its *constituents*. The major constituents of sentences can be isolated on an intuitive basis without any great difficulty. Think about the sentence below:

(1)   The daughter of a doddering old politician loved the son of Gertrude's first husband.

If you were asked to divide the longer sentence into the two most obvious word groups, it's unlikely that you'd do it this way:

The daughter of a doddering   old politician
                                       loved the son of
                                       Gertrude's first
                                       husband.

A more likely division would be:

| The daughter of a doddering old politician | loved the son of Gertrude's first husband. |

This division, or "passing," isolates from the rest of the sentence the constituent acting as subject. The constituent

The daughter of a doddering old politician

is a noun phrase, abbreviated as NP, as are the italicized sequences in the sentences below.

(2) *Ophelia* loved *Hamlet*.
(3) *The aging carpenter* sighed deeply.
(4) *Every day* passes more and more slowly.

The other main constituent of sentence (1) is a verb phrase:

loved the son of Gertrude's first husband

(abbreviated as VP). Current practice in discussions of sentence structure is to use a tree diagram to show the organization of constituents in sentences. The tree below asserts, in effect, that a sentence consists of a noun phrase and a verb phrase:

The basic tree diagram for the sentence

(5)   A tall philosopher denounced the behavioral psychologist.

is

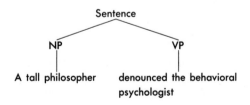

This tree is to be interpreted as asserting the following proper analysis of sentence (5).

Proper Analysis

1. *A tall philosopher* is a noun phrase.
2. *denounced the behavioral psychologist* is a verb phrase.
3. A noun phrase and a verb phrase are a sentence.

Note that the verb phrase

denounced the behavioral psychologist

consists of a verb, *denounced,* and also *the behavioral psychologist.*
What kind of constituent is the latter? It's made up of the same
kind of components as the noun phrase acting as subject:

a	tall	philosopher
the	behavioral	psychologist

It's a noun phrase also. It functions not as subject of the sentence,
however, but as object of the verb,

denounced the behavioral psychologist

The tree diagram below shows the more precise constituent structure

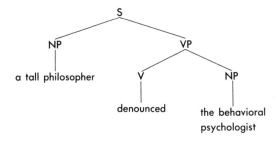

In giving the proper analysis now of the example sentence, you would
state the following:

Proper Analysis

1. *A tall philosopher* and *the behavioral psychologist* are noun
   phrases.
2. *denounced* is a verb.
3. The verb and the noun phrase following it are a verb phrase.
4. The noun phrase together with the verb phrase following it constitute a sentence.

Each of the noun phrases in sentence (5) contains three different kinds of constituents. The words *a* and *the*, usually called articles, are part of a larger class of words including *this, that, these, those, several, many of. Determiner* (abbreviated DET) is the broader term for all these words. Articles are an important subclass of determiners. The constituents *tall* and *behavioral* are adjectives (abbreviated ADJ). The words *philosopher* and *psychologist* are nouns, of course (abbreviated N). Now the tree diagram looks like this:

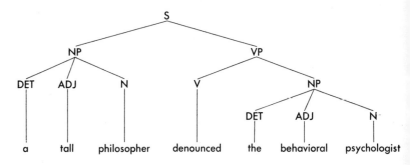

In theory, at least, noun phrases can be as long as you would like to make them — regardless of the role they play in a sentence. For instance, it is readily apparent that the subject noun phrase in sentence (6), (italicized for easy identification) could be extended infinitely.

(6) *The fact that he bothered to say that Harry thought that all of our troubles could be understood to have arisen from the suspicion that Mr. Dunwoodie, the barber, seemed to feel that . . . etc.* came as a total surprise to me.

Only in discussions of grammar do such monstrosities as the subject noun phrase of sentence (6) actually arise; though grammatical, the structure would be sufficient grounds for public denunciation in a composition course. Still, the point is an important one. Noun phrases are infinitely extendable in principle.

In the explanation of the infinite extendability lies a partial explanation of the speaker's ability to construct and comprehend an infinite number of sentences in his language. The major constituent, the sentence itself, may contain noun phrases which contain sentences which contain noun phrases which contain sentences which . . . In other words both sentences and noun phrases are recursive inside each other. Noun phrases are possible constituents of sentences and sentences are possible constituents of noun phrases. The sentence

A tall philosopher denounced the behavioral psychologist.

can itself be a constituent of a noun phrase, as is the noun phrase underlined in the sentence below.

The fact that a tall philosopher denounced the behavioral psychologist surprised me.

The constituent structure of the subject noun phrase of this sentence is this:

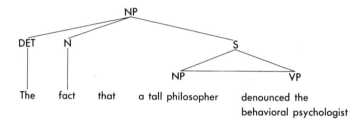

(Henceforth, constituent structure not essential to the discussion will be abbreviated by a triangle drawing.)

It's easy enough to make the intuitive determination that both *a tall philosopher* and *the behavioral psychologist* are constituents of the same kind, namely noun phrases. For instance, they can be interchanged without making the sentence ungrammatical:

The behavioral psychologist denounced the tall philosopher.

But this simple substitution test does not always work as well as it does here.

The most reliable tests for determining whether a group of words is or is not a constituent such as a noun phrase are *transformational tests,* since transformations affect different kinds of constituents in different ways. A transformation is a particular process of alteration by which one sentence structure is converted into another sentence structure without any change in the basic meaning. English makes use of a great many transformational rules. Some of these rearrange constituents, some delete constituents, some replace constituents with other constituents. One transformation which rearranges constituents is the PASSIVE Transformation.

The PASSIVE Transformation applies to *active* sentence structures such as that underlying the sentence

A tall philosopher denounced the behavioral psychologist.

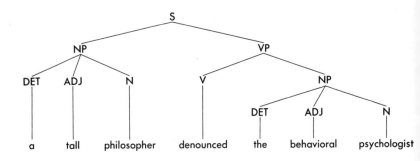

Among other things the PASSIVE Transformation interchanges the noun phrases. The original object noun phrase becomes a subject noun phrase, and the original subject noun phrase moves to the end of the sentence preceded by the preposition "by." (AUX stands for Auxiliary.)

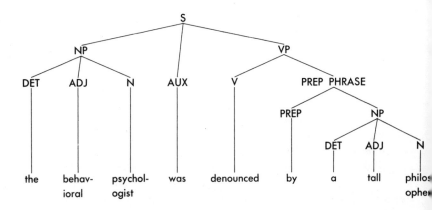

Thus, noun phrases can be defined in terms of transformations. Those constituents which are moved by the passive transformation are noun phrases. In other words, if a group of words in some active sentence

can be made to undergo the passive transformation, that group of words is a noun phrase.

Equally powerful tests for noun phrases are provided by transformations which move non-noun phrase constituents around noun phrases. One such transformation is the interrogative transformation relating declarative structures like

The befuddled old tyrant will do anything I tell him.

to interrogative structures like

Will the befuddled old tyrant do anything I tell him?

Roughly, the transformation converts a structure like

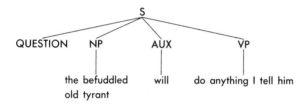

into:

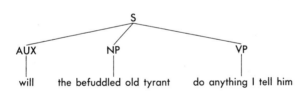

In English, transformations perform at least three basic functions. First, transformations exist which *move constituents around* in sentences. An example is the passive transformation. Second, transformations exist which *delete* constituent structure; for example, the transformation relating the sentence

John loved Mary and Bill loved Betty.

to

John loved Mary and Bill Betty.

Third, transformations exist which *substitute* one constituent for another, as in the transforming of

It is hard to see the shore

into

The shore is hard to see.

The overall function of transformations is to convert deep structures into surface structures. Normally, a deep structure will undergo an entire series of transformations before becoming a full surface structure. The basic meaning of sentences is implicit in their deep structures. These exist prior to the application of any transformations. Perhaps the most important characteristic of transformations in this grammatical framework is that transformations of sentences in no way alter the meaning of sentences. The meaning of sentences is preserved no matter how transformations modify the original sentence structure. Thus the sentences

A tall philosopher denounced the behavioral psychologist.
The behavioral psychologist was denounced by a tall philosopher.

mean logically exactly the same thing. However since the passive transformation effectively alters the focus of the active sentence, the surface meanings differ.

In summary, you have seen that sentences have both a meaning aspect and a form aspect, both representable by constituent structures. The basic meaning of a sentence is represented by its *deep structure*; the form of a sentence by its *surface structure*. Deep structures are converted into surface structures by rules of transformation, rules which move the constituents of constituent structures around and which delete them. Transformations do not alter the basic meaning of sentences. But although transformations do not alter the basic meaning of sentences, they do affect the surface meaning. Choosing an active over a passive is a stylistic choice.

Shakespeare *might* have written

The youth of the realm have most traitorously been corrupted by thee in erecting a grammar-school . . . One will prove to thy face that thou hast men about thee that usually talk of a noun and a verb, and such abominable words as can be endured by no Christian ear.

However he actually used the passive transformation once where it is not used above and did not use the passive transformation where it is twice used above. Basically, Shakespeare's version, the one following, is synonymous with that above:

> Thou has most traitorously corrupted the youth of the realm in erecting a grammar-school . . . It will be proved to thy face that thou hast men about thee that usually talk of a noun and a verb, and such abominable words as no Christian ear can endure to hear.

> Shakespeare, Henry VI, Part II, IV, vii

Finding out more about the effect of the transformation difference is basically finding out more about the contribution of style to meaning.

Exercises for Chapter Three

1. Draw constituent structure tree diagrams for the sentences below:
   (a) The flaming torch touched the curtain.
   (b) Time elapsed.
   (c) That fellow will hurt himself.
2. Give the proper analysis for each of the sentences in exercise 1.
3. Explain how the passive transformation provides a test for noun phrases. Illustrate your discussion with a carefully chosen example.
4. Give two examples each of transformations which
   (a) permute constituents
   (b) delete constituents
   and one example of a transformation which replaces constituents.
5. Describe the function of transformations in human language.
6. Choose a suitable short passage from any novel or short story and turn all active sentences into passive sentences wherever possible. Then comment on the effect. Are passive sentences necessarily worse than active ones?

BIBLIOGRAPHY

CHOMSKY, NOAM. *Language and Mind.* New York: Harcourt, 1968, Chapter 3.

————. *Aspects of the Theory of Syntax.* Cambridge, Mass.: M.I.T. Press, 1965, pp. 15–25.

JACOBS, RODERICK A. and PETER S. ROSENBAUM. *An Introduction to Transformational Grammar: Grammars 1 and 2.* Waltham, Mass.: Ginn, 1970.

LYONS, JOHN. *Introduction to Theoretical Linguistics.* Cambridge, England: Cambridge University Press 1968, pp. 210–225.

Abstractness and Transformational Ordering

4

The causes why [our English tung] hath not as yet bene thoroughlie perceaved, ar, the hope and despare of such, as haue either thought vpon it, and not delt in it, or that haue delt in it, but not rightlie thought vpon it.

Richard Mulcaster (1582)

Transformations, such as the passive transformation, play a dynamic role in language. And such dynamic functions exist solely in order to relate form to meaning. A *transformational grammar,* the technical term for this sort of description of language, postulates abstract objects, that is, deep structures, which underlie the sentences of all human languages. The precise nature of these deep structures is still being investigated. However, as you have already seen, deep structures enable linguists to account at least partially for such well-known properties of language as synonymy, ambiguity, and other complex semantic relationships understood by native speakers. Such deep structures are not sentences; they are abstract entities realized as sentences only through the application of transformations which convert them into surface structures.

The two surface structures shown as sentences below have much semantic content in common, but one major difference is apparent.

Norman Mailer will write another novel.
Will Norman Mailer write another novel?

In both sentences *Norman Mailer* is the subject noun phrase, *another novel* is the object noun phrase, and the verb is the same form of *write* together with the auxiliary word *will.* The physical difference lies in the position of *will* and the end punctuation (or, in speech, the intonation). A grammarian might suggest the following tree as a picture of what the two sentences have in common:

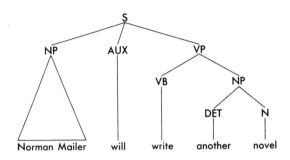

This is acceptable as an approximate deep structure for the declarative sentence; but it is not an adequate representation of the interrogative sentence. Since deep structures always reflect the meaning of sentences, the surface structures of two sentences having different meanings would not share the same deep structure. If they had the same deep structure the surface structures defined from this deep structure would be synonymous. The declarative sentence makes the assertion that Mailer will in fact write another novel. The interrogative sentence makes no such claim. The answer to the question could be:

Yes. He told me it will be about Vietnam.

but it could just as well be:

No. He's just writing two articles for *The New York Review*.

Indeed linguists often call such questions *yes–no questions.*

Since the function of a deep structure tree is to present the information needed for semantic interpretation, the tree shown above must be amended to include some kind of notation that it is in question whether (or not) Norman Mailer will write another novel. In Chapter Two, the tree for one yes–no question sentence did present a special notation. It included the element QUESTION, as does the more accurate version of the deep structure of the Norman Mailer question sentence presented following.

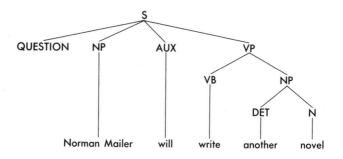

This tree provides for a question interpretation of the yes–no sentence through the positing of the abstract element QUESTION as a constituent of the deep structure underlying the question:

Will Norman Mailer write another novel?

The tree is an abstract representation of the constituents and structural relationships necessary to explain the semantic interpretation assigned to this sentence by native speakers of English. The symbol QUESTION has no physical reality in the final sentence. It has no sound waves that can be measured on oscilloscopes; it has no directly corresponding neurophysical operations in the brain (as far as is currently known), detectable in electroencephalograms. Still, abstract models such as these reflect an important kind of mental reality, one involving what a native speaker of a particular language knows intuitively about a particular class of sentences in his language, knowledge that enables him to produce and understand it under just the appropriate circumstances.

The elements of such a tree have transformational consequences. By the time the string shown in the tree above has reached the surface structure level, the order of the elements will have been changed and the element QUESTION will have been removed. The auxiliary *will* will no longer follow the first noun phrase, as it does in the declarative sentence

Norman Mailer will write another novel.

In the yes–no question, *will* finally precedes the first noun phrase (the subject in both deep and surface structures). The transformational process applying to the deep structure shifts the auxiliary word *will* around to the left of the subject noun phrase. When this happens, the element QUESTION is automatically deleted. As you will see shortly, there are times when this constituent is not deleted, when it actually appears in the surface structure as a particular word. Still, the proximity of *will*, and other auxiliary words like it, to the QUESTION element seems to cause the deletion of this abstract constituent.

The QUESTION element is a kind of trigger for the QUESTION Transformation. When the QUESTION element is not present in the deep structure, the declarative form of a sentence results. When it *is* present, the interrogative sentence is produced. In this way the grammar of English prevents the application of this transformation to deep structures not interpreted semantically as questions. Now consider the one case where the QUESTION element is actually spelled out in the surface structure. This case is that of the indirect question. If the Norman Mailer question sentence is embedded after *He asked*, the element QUESTION is realized as *whether:*

He asked whether Norman Mailer would write another novel.

In earlier forms of English, *whether* occurs in direct questions:

Hwaeðer ӡe nu secan gold on treowum? [Do you now seek gold on trees?]

King Alfred, *Cons. Phil.*, 73.24[1]

Much the same kind of description will account for the semantic difference between negative and affirmative sentences:

Norman Mailer will write another novel.
Norman Mailer will not write another novel.

The second sentence contains an additional word, a word which is critical to your understanding of the meaning. Once again, the deep structures of the two sentences are alike in many respects, but the second must somehow convey the notion "it is not the case that" or "it is false that." The element NEGATIVE is often used to characterize this interpretation.

---

[1] We thank Dr. Elizabeth Traugott of the University of California at Berkeley for this example.

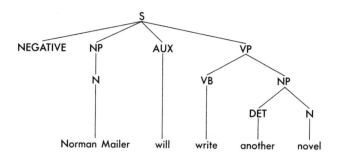

Here the negative element serves as a trigger for the NEGATIVE Transformation. This transformation takes the element NEGATIVE and shifts it to the position after the auxiliary.

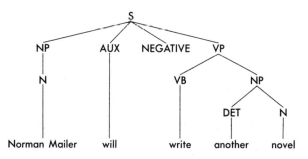

By a later transformation, this abstract constituent is transformed into the word *not*.

Note that both transformations are concerned with the auxiliary. The QUESTION Transformation shifts the auxiliary around the subject noun phrase. The NEGATIVE Transformation shifts the negative element after the auxiliary where it becomes *not*. A further transformation is applied optionally. The CONTRACTION Transformation converts

Norman Mailer will not write another novel.

into

Norman Mailer won't write another novel.

But you might wonder what happens when the sentence appears to have no auxiliary, as in

Norman Mailer wrote another novel.

This sentence is presumed to have an auxiliary in its deep structure:

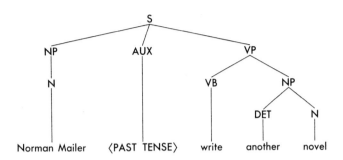

(The angle brackets ⟨ ⟩ are used to indicate that the enclosed material is not a constituent, but a semantic feature or property of a constituent. Here ⟨PAST TENSE⟩ is the property accounting for the past time interpretation of the sentence.) When ⟨PAST⟩ is incorporated with *write* the surface structure form becomes *wrote*. If the tense were ⟨PRESENT⟩, then the verb would become either *writes* or *write*, depending on the singularity or plurality of the surface subject.

Words like *will, shall, can,* and *may* together with their past tense forms *would, should, could,* and *might* are known as *modal* auxiliaries. The first two (and the contraction *'ll*) followed by a verb are used in English to form what is sometimes called the *future tense*. It is now more customary to use the term *tense* to refer only to the *verb* forms of a language. English has only past and present tense verb forms. Latin, Sanskrit, Greek, and French have many more. This more modern usage of the term syntactic "tense" has the advantage of separating the notion of syntactic *tense* from that of *time*.

After all, tense does not correspond to time in sentences like:

Malenkov jumps a foot in the air whenever I yell at him.
He will be opening the letter now.
Dr. Selwyn goes to Dorset next week.
So that copper tells me that my mini-car is parked in the wrong place. So I picks it up and carries it into Whitehall Place.

When the auxiliary is not a modal, and the auxiliary constituent immediately precedes a VP, a transformation deletes the auxiliary. However, when a transformation such as the CONTRACTION,

QUESTION, or NEGATIVE Transformation causes some other constituent to intervene between a non-modal auxiliary word and the VP, then the auxiliary is not deleted. Instead it is realized as a word in the surface structure, a form of the word "do." "Do," with its other forms *does* and *did,* is a *non-modal* auxiliary. These observations explain why the interrogative sentence corresponding to

Norman Mailer wrote another novel.

is

***Did* Norman Mailer write another novel?**

and the negative sentence is

Norman Mailer *did* not write another novel.

The following example shows what happens in greater detail. When a deep structure contains no modal, the feature ⟨−MODAL⟩ is a property of the deep structure auxiliary.

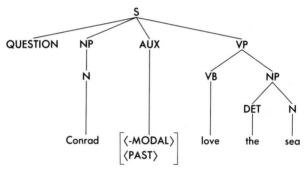

If the above deep structure did not include QUESTION, the tense element ⟨PAST⟩ would be incorporated into *love* and the entire auxiliary constituent would then be deleted from the surface structure.

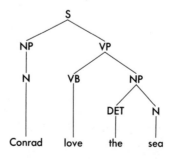

Conrad loved the sea.

But, since QUESTION is in the deep structure, the QUESTION Transformation is triggered. This shifts the auxiliary to the front of the sentence.

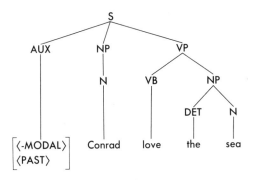

To be incorporated into the verb, PAST[2] must be right next to the verb. Since it isn't, and since the auxiliary is non-modal, the auxiliary takes on the form *did:*

Did Conrad love the sea?

Negative sentences are generated similarly. In the tree the NEG-

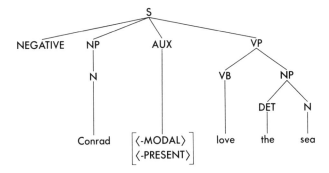

ATIVE element triggers the NEGATIVE Transformation. This transformation shifts the NEGATIVE element to the position in between the auxiliary and the VP.

---

[2] Since there are only two *tenses* in English, the present and the past (or non-present), the present tense feature will henceforth be shown as ⟨+present⟩ and the past as ⟨−present⟩.

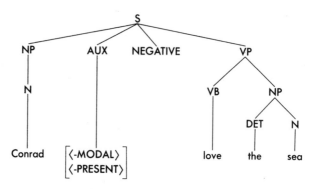

Now the NEGATIVE element prevents the tense from being incorporated into the verb (producing *loved*). Instead, a form of the non-modal *do* has to be employed. The negative is realized as *not*, so the surface structure is

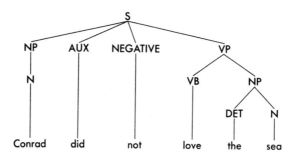

If this structure is viewed as an intermediate structure, not as the surface structure, the *not* is converted into *n't* by the CONTRACTION Transformation, which also adjoins the *n't* to *did*. The surface structure is now

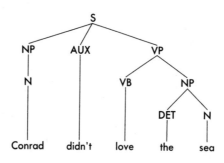

Deep structures, then, are abstract representations of the constituents and relationships available for semantic interpretation. The transformations, which are meaning-preserving, convert deep structures into surface structures, usually through successive transformations of structure into surface structure. The transformations must often be applied in a particular order. For example, the CONTRACTION Transformation must be applied after the *not* has been introduced by the NEGATIVE Transformation. The transformation incorporating the tense into the verb (the TENSE INCORPORATION Transformation) cannot be applied before the NEGATIVE or QUESTION Transformations or strings like

　* Conrad do not loved the sea

and

　* do Conrad loved the sea?

would be generated.

Can you see why? Tense incorporation requires that the verb follow a non-modal auxiliary in sequence. Furthermore, this arrangement will always be true of deep structures, structures to which no transformations have applied. Unless some constituent is somehow placed between this auxiliary and the verb, tense incorporation will take place. Since we know that tense incorporation does not occur in such sentences as

　Conrad did not love the sea.

and

　Did Conrad love the sea?

the NEGATIVE and QUESTION Transformations must apply before the TENSE INCORPORATION Transformation, thereby rendering the latter inapplicable. Thus, these transformations are ordered.

Exercises for Chapter Four

1. Here are two English transformations
   (a) The REFLEXIVE Transformation: If the subject and object noun phrases of a sentence refer to the same entity, then the object noun phrase is transformed into a reflexive pronoun.

Napoleon thought highly of Napoleon ⇒
Napoleon thought highly of himself

(b) The IMPERATIVE Transformation: An imperative sentence is formed by the deletion of the pronoun *you* when in subject position.

You drop dead ⇒
Drop dead

Using the following sentence and non-sentence (to which both transformations have applied) as evidence, figure out the ordering of these two transformations and justify your conclusions.
(a) Behave yourself!
(b) * Behave you.

2. Draw deep structure trees for the following sentences:
   (a) Did Smith smash the car?
   (b) Muscles don't atrophy.
   (c) Vandals stole the money.
   (d) I will not touch it.

3. Explain how the NEGATIVE and QUESTION Transformations can be used as tests to determine whether a word or sequence of words is a noun phrase. Illustrate your explanation with examples.

BIBLIOGRAPHY

CHOMSKY, NOAM. *Aspects of the Theory of Syntax.* Cambridge, Mass.: M.I.T. Press, 1965, pp. 63–79, 135–137, 140–147.

JACOBS, RODERICK A. and PETER S. ROSENBAUM. *Readings in English Transformational Grammar.* Waltham, Mass.: Ginn, 1968, Chapters 3, 4, and 5.

KATZ, J. and PAUL M. POSTAL. *An Integrated Theory of Linguistic Descriptions.* Cambridge, Mass.: M.I.T. Press, 1964, pp. 74–78, 84–89.

Sentence Embedding, Transformations, and Style

5

After a lecture on the solar system, William James was approached by an old lady who claimed she had a superior theory to the one described by James.

"We don't live on a ball rotating around the sun," she said. "We live on a crust of earth on the back of a giant turtle."

Not wishing to demolish this absurd argument with the massive scientific evidence at his command, James decided to dissuade his opponent gently.

"If your theory is correct, madam, what does this turtle stand on?"

"You're a very clever man, Mr. James, and that's a good question, but I can answer that. The first turtle stands on the back of a second, far larger, turtle."

"But what does this second turtle stand on?" James asked patiently.

The old lady crowed triumphantly, "It's no use, Mr. James—it's turtles all the way down."

Reported by J. R. Ross in his
Ph. D. thesis, *Constraints on
Variables in Syntax,* 1967

One of the more important features of all human language is that there is no grammatical limit to the length of a sentence. Even though very long sentences are rare in actual language performance, the processes by which sentences could be made infinitely long are always very much in evidence. One of these processes is *conjunction,* a term which refers to the joining of two or more sentences. The second process is *subordination,* which refers to the *embedding* of a sentence inside another sentence. It is this phenomenon of sentence embedding which is the focus of this chapter.

The following sentence illustrates a very common case of subordination.

> *The fact that he did not know what politics meant* pained Stephen Daedalus.

The first point to note is that the string *The fact that he did not know what politics meant* is a noun phrase, as the passive and interrogative versions of this sentence show:

> Stephen Daedalus was pained by *the fact that he did not know what politics meant*. Did *the fact that he did not know what politics meant* pain Stephen Daedalus?

The second point of importance is that this noun phrase itself contains the sentence *he did not know what politics meant*. The noun phrase in the sentences above thus consists of three primary constituents: a determiner, *the*, a noun, *fact*, and a sentence, *he did not know what politics meant*. The structure of such a noun phrase is given in the tree diagram below.

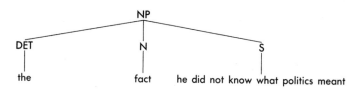

The word "that" as it is used in the noun phrase *the fact that he did not know what politics meant* serves the purpose of giving a special mark to a sentence embedded inside a noun phrase. This word is called a *complementizing morpheme* or simply a *complementizer*. This term derives from the general linguistic term referring to that special case of subordination where sentences are embedded inside noun phrases: *noun phrase complementation*. The embedded sentence, *he did not know what politics meant*, is a constituent of a noun phrase. It functions as the complement of that noun phrase. Hence, the word *that* is known as a complementizer.

Only certain kinds of abstract nouns can fit into the position of "fact" words like *idea, news, belief:*

The news that snow is expected worries us. *The idea that you should want to go out and make your fortune* could not be surprising to any reasonable adult. *The belief that democracy will survive* sustains much of the Western World.

Up to this point you have been looking at noun phrase structures containing not only an embedded sentence but also a determiner and a noun. Now compare the following two sentences.

(1)   *The fact that you can't look after your own affairs* worries me.
(2)   *That you can't look after your own affairs* worries me.

The second of these two sentences has for a subject what appears to be only a sentence with a complementizer, *that you can't look after your own affairs.* But how can a noun phrase exist without a noun as a primary constituent? This question can be answered satisfactorily only on the assumption that there is a difference between the deep structures of sentences and the surface, because, as you will shortly see, the deep structure of sentence (2) does indeed contain a noun as a primary constituent. For various transformational reasons, this noun disappears under certain circumstances in the surface structure.

Consider the following sentences:

(2)   *That you can't look after your own affairs* worries me.
(3)   *It* worries me *that you can't look after your own affairs.*

These sentences are synonymous. Furthermore, they have enough in common syntactically for a linguist to suspect that they might have identical deep structures. But what deep structure could these two sentences share?

Suppose that the subject noun phrase in the deep structure of both sentences consists of a pronoun, which is nothing more than a special type of noun, and a complement sentence, as in the following tree diagram:

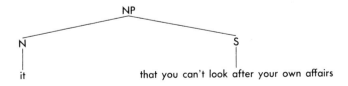

To be sure, surface structures such as

(4)   * *It that you can't look after your own affairs* worries me

are ungrammatical in English. However, suppose that whenever a structure like the one above occurs, one of two transformations must apply. The first such transformation can be described thus:

> Whenever a sentence follows the pronoun "it" in a noun phrase, the option exists of moving that sentence to the end of the sentence in which it is embedded.

This transformation, called the EXTRAPOSITION Transformation, converts the structure represented by the ungrammatical string

(4)   * *It that you can't look after your own affairs* worries me

into the fully grammatical sentence

(3)   *It* worries me *that you can't look after your own affairs.*

The second transformation works as follows:

> Whenever the conditions for the extraposition transformation exist, but this transformation is not applied, then the pronoun *it* must be deleted.

This transformation, the IT DELETION Transformation, converts the ungrammatical structure

(4)   * *It that you can't look after your own affairs* worries me

into the grammatical sentence

(2)   *That you can't look after your own affairs* worries me.

Thus the assumption of two transformations, the EXTRAPOSITION and IT DELETION Transformations, allows sentences (2) and (3) to share common deep structures. Since they do share common deep structures, the fact that these two sentences have exactly the same logical meaning is explained.

There are many formal linguistic reasons for this formulation, reasons which justify the existence of such strange looking noun phrase complement structures. English still contains a number of frequently used constructions in which *it* is followed by some complement sentence.

(5)   I'll see to *it that he comes on time.*
(6)   She dislikes *it that you should think so poorly of her parents.*

It is particularly interesting that extraposed sentences appear to be easier to understand than those to which IT DELETION has been applied. The sentence below illustrates this rather well.

(7)   It pained him that he did not know what politics meant and where the universe ended.

Had the IT DELETION Transformation been applied instead of EXTRAPOSITION, the result would have been

(8)   That he did not know what politics meant and where the universe ended pained him.

which is understandable but certainly a little clumsier. This distinction becomes even clearer in the light of James Joyce's more complex original sentence.

(9)   It pained him that he did not know well what politics meant and that he did not know where the universe ended.

James Joyce, *Portrait of the Artist as a Young Man*

If EXTRAPOSITION had not been carried out for Joyce's sentences, the result of IT DELETION would have been indigestible though technically still grammatical:

(10)   That he did not know well what politics meant and that he did not know where the universe ended pained him.

So, although transformations preserve the basic meaning of a sentence structure, the choice of one transformational route rather than another can have important stylistic consequences.

It has already been noted that the PASSIVE Transformation generates sentences basically synonymous with their active counterparts, but differing slightly in focus. A skilled writer may exploit this subtle difference occasionally, but unfortunate freshman composition students may be burned at the stake for overusing the passive construction. Yet another transformation involving noun phrases also affects focus. This one is called the CLEFT SENTENCE Transformation. The sentence

(11)   The fear that Ledbetter would murder the English language drove Dr. Chesterwether insane.

has a cleft counterpart

(12)   What drove Dr. Chesterwether insane was the fear that Ledbetter would murder the English language.

The CLEFT SENTENCE Transformation involves, very roughly speaking, three basic steps:

1. place *what* at the beginning of the string
2. place the appropriate form of *be* at the end of the string
3. shift a noun phrase to the end of the string

Since this transformation only works if the constituent shifted in step 3 really is a noun phrase, the CLEFT SENTENCE Transformation can actually be a good test for distinguishing noun phrases.

Suppose you must apply this transformation to

(13)   The loud sneeze destroyed the temporary lecture hall.

The first step converts it into

(14)   * What the loud sneeze destroyed the lecture hall

and the second into

(15)   * What the loud sneeze destroyed the lecture hall was

In the final step you have to shift a noun phrase to the end. Since there are two, *the loud sneeze* and *the lecture hall,* there are two possible sentences:

(16)   What destroyed the lecture hall was the loud sneeze.

and

(17)   What the loud sneeze destroyed was the lecture hall.

The CLEFT SENTENCE Transformation, though preserving logical synonymy, does focus the attention on the particular noun phrase shifted to the end. In the first of the last two example sentences, the focus is on the loud sneeze whereas, in the second, focus is on the lecture hall. Moreover in the first it is *presupposed* that something has destroyed the lecture hall. This fact is taken for granted and the burden of the sentence is on the cause of the destruction. But in the second, the presupposition is that the loud sneeze has destroyed something and the sentence focuses on what was destroyed. Cleft sentences, like passives, can therefore be very useful.

Look now at two passages which exploit these transformations to achieve interesting surface effects and to create a style with its own meaning. The two passages are basically synonymous. But the choices made between alternative transformations result in the additional dimension of meaning that we have called surface meaning. Style is the result of linguistic choice and surface meaning is the result of style.

> And yet, that there *was* something which all black men held in common became clear as the debate wore on. They held in common their precarious, their unutterably painful relation to the white world. They held in common the necessity to remake the world in their own image, to impose this image on the world. . . . The vision of the world, and of themselves which other people held would no longer control them. In sum, black men held in common their ache to come into the world as men.

> And yet, it became clear as the debate wore on, that there *was* something which all black men held in common. . . . What they held in common was their precarious, their unutterably painful relation to the white world. What they held in common was the necessity to remake the world in their own image, to impose this image on the world, and no longer be controlled by the vision of the world and of themselves, held by other people. What, in sum, black men held in common was their ache to come into the world as men.

Both passages are concerned with a particular state of mind common to all black men, it is claimed. In the past, blacks have been acted upon rather than acting on others; they have accepted a view of life formulated by others and have thereby been emasculated. Because of this they share the need to assert themselves as men by reversing the older passive relationship.

The first sentence of the first passage is hard to digest because the writer has chosen not to extrapose:

(18) And yet, that there was something which all black men held in common became clear as the debate wore on.

The use of the EXTRAPOSITION Transformation in the second passage yields a more readable alternative:

(19) And yet, it became clear as the debate wore on, that there *was* something which all black men held in common.

This alternative seems more readable. What about the rest of the first passage? The CLEFT SENTENCE Transformation could have been used to focus on the object noun phrases of each verb by shifting that noun phrase to the end of its sentences, right after the copula. This would spotlight the noun phrases:

1. their precarious, their unutterably painful relation to the white world
2. the necessity to remake the world in their own image . . .
3. their ache to come into the world as men

These show a mounting scale of desired activity, culminating in that desired state of coming "as men." The cleft versions should enhance this with structures like this:

(20) What they held in common was their precarious
(21) What they held in common was the necessity to . . .

This is what has happened in the second version. The second and third sentences of the first already have nicely parallel subjects and verbs, but the fourth sentence has the blacks consigned to the object position at the end of a long sentence. In the second passage, the passive transformation reverses the subjects and objects of this sentence without changing the sense. Now *they* is the subject and the long noun phrase beginning with *the vision* . . . is the object:

(22) They would no longer be controlled by the vision of the world and themselves which other people held.

Since the second, third, and fourth sentences all have *they* as subject, they can be joined together with an *and.* But since the new sentence would be rather long, the writer preferred just to conjoin the third and fourth sentences and keep the parallelism of *what they held in common. . . .*

So the third and fourth sentences are now one:

(23) What they held in common was the necessity to remake the world in their own image, to impose this image on the world, and no longer be controlled by the vision of the world and themselves which other people held.

The sentence contrasts the desired black activeness in the first half with the past black passiveness in the second half. And the active theme is reinforced by active constructions in the first half and passive constructions in the second half. In fact this isn't quite correct since the last clause, *which other people held,* is, unlike the one in the second passage, still active. So a change to *which was held by other people* and deletion of the unnecessary *which was* (this is a common transformation in English) achieves the final effect.

The second version has greater coherence and strength. The last three sentences each beginning with *what* (suggesting an implied question) end in a powerful series *white world, other people,* and finally, *men.* This last noun emphasizes the normality and humanness of a desire shared not just by blacks or by whites but by all men. Note that the presuppositional effect of the cleft rule modifies the *held in common* idea. The writer takes it for granted that these black men shared the same need, a need which, he implies later, all men share and should therefore understand. To make this powerful plea, James Baldwin used the second of these two versions in his book, *Nobody Knows My Name.*[1]

But in one respect Baldwin may have overdone the transformational manipulation. His long penultimate sentence is very cleverly constructed. The two clauses with active verbs *to remake* and *to impose* match the active control desired. They are balanced by the long clause with two passives *be controlled* and *held by other people.* This matches the present passive situation of the blacks. But the surface meaning does not quite come through as intended. Readers often find the sentences hard to read because of the conjoining of active and passive verbs, *to impose . . . and no longer be controlled by.* It is difficult for the reader to shift gears quickly enough to enter smoothly into a world where the previous semantic subject is not the semantic object.

Baldwin's passage is here so elaborately structured that the desired message is partially obscured by an additional surface meaning — that the writer is somewhat inappropriately and excessively concerned with the formal design of his sentences. The style is thus no longer an apparently inevitable and therefore unobtrusive result of the interaction between the writer and his subject matter.

Exercises for Chapter Five

1. Draw deep structure trees in as much detail as you can for the following sentences:

    (a) It incensed me that my manager didn't appreciate my work.

    (b) It isn't known by the meteorologist whether it will rain.

---

[1] James Baldwin. *Nobody Knows My Name.* New York: Dell, 1961, p. 35.

  (c) Is she frightened by the fact that Harry has nightmares?

  (d) That the barometer is rising suggests that the waves will subside.

2. Explain how the deep structures you drew in the first exercise become surface structures.

3. Make up a list of ten nouns which can appear in noun phrases with noun phrase complements (for example, "fact"), and illustrate each one in a sentence. Do not use any of the nouns mentioned in this chapter.

4. In which of the following sentences is the word "that" used as a complementizer?

  (a) It would seem that he just has to be allowed to proceed.

  (b) Critics think that picture playing on 34th Street is a loser.

  (c) Considering what you seem to feel about that, you ought to just leave well enough alone.

  (d) That things will get worse before they get better is a gross and pessimistic overgeneralization.

  (e) A tree that has suffered in recent years is the elm.

  (f) That stinks!

5. In your own words, construct a short paragraph explaining why it is that the following three sentences have exactly the same logical meaning.

  (a) It disturbs me that you can never be on time.

  (b) I am disturbed that you can never be on time.

  (c) That you can never be on time disturbs me.

  To make your explanation complete, you will have to formulate a transformation not discussed in the chapter. Be sure to identify this transformation and how it works. (*Hint:* In most cases, a subject noun phrase moved to the end of the sentence by the passive transformation will be preceded there by the word "by.")

6. Comment on the differences between the odd and even members of each pair of sentences below.

  (1a) Huck admired Jim greatly. This led him to change his attitude toward a man he had once regarded as a chattel. Since he was able to do this, this suggests he had not been fully indoctrinated by Pap.

  (2a) Huck's great admiration for Jim led him to change his attitude toward a man he had once regarded as a chattel. His ability to do this suggests that he had not been fully indoctrinated by Pap.

  (1b) The governor approved the law, denying that he was responsible for introducing it. This enraged the younger voters.

They demanded that the law be repealed by the legislature, but that only made the legislators more obstinate.

(2b) The governor's approval of the law and his denial of any responsibility for its introduction enraged the younger voters. But their demand for the repeal of the law by the legislature only made the legislators more obstinate.

(1c) The waves crashed. The wind howled. The lifeboat rocked perilously. All this drove us into a state of frenzied terror.

(2c) The crashing of the waves, the howling of the wind, and the perilous rocking of the lifeboat all drove us into a state of frenzied terror.

BIBLIOGRAPHY

CHOMSKY, NOAM. "Deep Structure, Surface Structure and Semantic Interpretation" in Jakobovits, L. and D. Steinberg, *Semantics: An Interdisciplinary Reader.* Champaign: Illinois University Press, 1970.

JACOBS, RODERICK A. and PETER S. ROSENBAUM. *English Transformational Grammar.* Waltham, Mass.: Ginn, 1968, Chapters 7, 20, and 21.

OHMANN, RICHARD. "Literature as Sentences," in *College English,* Volume 27, No. 4 (January 1966), pages 261–267.

Features and the Representation of Meaning

6

What is the metre of the dictionary?
The size of genesis? The short spark's gender?

Dylan Thomas

From one point of view the question as to whether cats are human or not is a linguistic question. English reserves a special relative pronoun *who* for human beings. Everything else — animal, vegetable, or mineral; abstract or concrete — must be content with *which* or the neutral pronoun *that.* So speakers of those prestigious English dialects associated with educated white society might say

(1) The boy who stood on the burning deck

or

(2) The tree which stood by the Animal Rescue Center

but would regard as slipshod or downright ungrammatical

(3) *The boy which stood on the burning deck[1]

No dialects of English have been described as allowing

(4) *The tree who stood by the Animal Rescue Center

For many speakers of English, the sentence

---

[1] Though *which* was used earlier for human nouns even in the most prestigious dialects; for example,

Our Father *which* art in heaven . . .

The *which* here is not a function of godhead, of course.

(5)   The cat who ate the ham ran that way.

is not acceptable unless either *which* or *that* replaces *who*. Those who dote on cats are more likely to accept the *who*. Treat the cat as human by giving it a name and even the most dogmatic cat hater has to use *who* in sentences like

(6)   Their cat Archibald, who just hates fish, is presently on a steak and lobster diet.

Check your own intuitions as to the use of *who* for ants, bees, and mosquitoes. The tree maniac whose best friend is a birch tree might call it John and therefore use *who*. We would, if we accepted the name, be forced into accepting:

(7)   John, who stands outside his front door, is having a problem with aphids.

So the world view of the speaker may determine in part the acceptability of certain utterances. One current issue in theoretical syntax is whether there needs to be a sharp distinction between semantic anomaly and ungrammaticality. Nouns like *woman, masseuse,* and *queen* are pronominalized as *she*, not *he*. Nouns without this female feature are not normally modified by adjectives such as *pregnant*. Inanimate nouns like *house* cannot normally be the subject of verbs like *try:*

(8)   Her house tried to look neat.

except in metaphorical or highly stylized discourse. The use of grammatical terms here may be misleading. As McCawley has pointed out,[2] a paranoid who says

(9)   My toothbrush is alive and is trying to kill me.

is not observing grammatical restrictions requiring animate subjects for *alive* and *trying*. The difference between his usage and ours corresponds exactly to a difference in beliefs regarding relationships with inanimate objects. A man uttering the example sentence above should be referred to a psychiatric clinic, not to a remedial English course.

---

[2] James D. McCawley, "Where Do Noun Phrases Come From?" in Jacobs and Rosenbaum, *Readings in English Transformational Grammar*. Waltham, Mass.: Ginn, 1970.

The comment of Shakespeare's Theseus is apt at this point:

The lunatic, the lover and the poet
Are of imagination all compact.

A Midsummer Night's Dream

for the poet may use language to exploit such worlds:

(10)   Will the sunflower turn to us, will the clematis
Stray down, bend to us; tendril and spray
Clutch and cling?
Chill
Fingers of yew be curled
Down on us? After the kingfisher's wing
Has answered light to light, and is silent,
     the light is still
At the still point of the turning world.

T. S. Eliot, *Burnt Norton*

Verbs like *snarl, enjoy, admire,* and *devour* all require animate subjects. If a non-animate noun phrase is used:

(11)   Two thousand trumpets snarled from the walls of Troy.

the literary phenomenon *personification* manifests itself. The trumpets take on an animate quality. *Personification* here, however, is hardly a good term, since the trumpets are beast-like rather than "person-like."

Other features of words besides animateness are of importance here. The word *life* is not an animate or concrete noun. In non-metaphorical language it does not serve as the subject of active verbs like *announce* or the object of verbs like *scrub.* So when T. S. Eliot writes

(12)   I have measured out my life in coffee spoons.

he is using such violations of the linguistic–semantic norm to create a different world view where the incongruity of associating significant life experience with coffee spoons suggests a weary disillusion with a half-life of rootless triviality.

Between the words

a . . . ago

a time noun is expected: *week, month, second.* But if a non-time noun is used, differing worlds are fused:

a grief ago

A world view is created in which life is a sad, perhaps tragic business. The word *grief* has taken on the time-measurement quality. Life is not just a stringing together of minutes, hours, days, years; it can be measured off in griefs — as well as in coffee spoons.

So words are not simple grammatical objects with simple characteristics or features. The sounds that make them up are complexes of acoustic and articulatory features. Words represent complexes of real-world properties. Books are solid objects. They can't be poured into bottles. Some purely grammatical and lexical properties also are associated with the word *book*. For example you know that *book* can act as either a noun or a verb. When a noun, it is a common noun, unlike the word *Patricia*. Its singular form, unlike *Patricia*, requires an article before it, like *a, the, this,* or *that*.

Such properties: nounhood, common (versus proper), concrete (versus abstract), animate (versus inanimate), human (versus non-human) have to be referred to often in a grammar. One useful notation is known as feature notation. If a noun is a common noun, it is shown as "plus common," that is, ⟨+ common⟩. If the noun is a proper noun, the noun is represented with ⟨− common⟩. Abstract nouns are ⟨− concrete⟩, whereas concrete nouns are ⟨+ concrete⟩. The choice of the name for a feature, for example, *concreteness* rather than *abstractness*, is an arbitrary one. Such features form an important part of the grammatical description of any language.

So, in addition to providing rules for producing deep structures and for converting them into surface structures, the grammar of English embodies a *lexicon* from which words and affixes are selected and placed in the appropriate places in the deep structure tree. Here is represented the lexical knowledge of the native speaker. The nouns *book, boy,* and *faith* would have as part of their lexical entries the following information:

book	boy	faith
$\begin{bmatrix} \langle +\text{N} \rangle \\ \langle +\text{common} \rangle \\ \langle +\text{concrete} \rangle \\ \langle -\text{animate} \rangle \\ \langle -\text{human} \rangle \end{bmatrix}$	$\begin{bmatrix} \langle +\text{N} \rangle \\ \langle +\text{common} \rangle \\ \langle +\text{concrete} \rangle \\ \langle +\text{animate} \rangle \\ \langle +\text{human} \rangle \end{bmatrix}$	$\begin{bmatrix} \langle +\text{N} \rangle \\ \langle +\text{common} \rangle \\ \langle -\text{concrete} \rangle \\ \langle -\text{animate} \rangle \\ \langle -\text{human} \rangle \end{bmatrix}$

These entries contain some redundant information. Since *book* is inanimate, it is obviously non-human. Since *boy* is human, it is obviously animate. And since *faith* is abstract, that is, ⟨−concrete⟩, it must be inanimate and non-human. In other words, certain properties are predictable from others. The lexical entries could therefore be pruned of some features.

There are a number of other features with syntactic import. For instance, the cluster of features for nouns will indicate *number*, that is, whether they are ⟨+ singular⟩ or ⟨− singular⟩, since this feature determines not only the presence or absence of the plural suffix *s* but also the form of verbs when the noun is the subject of a sentence. Furthermore *person* — first, second, or third — also plays a major role. Regular nouns are all third person, ⟨+ III⟩, but pronouns may be first, second, or third. Actually a pronoun may have more than one person feature. Here are two partially specified entries for *we*.

$$
\text{we} \qquad\qquad\qquad\qquad \text{we}
$$

$$
\begin{bmatrix} \langle +\text{N} \rangle \\ \langle +\text{pronoun} \rangle \\ \langle +\text{I} \rangle \\ \langle -\text{II} \rangle \\ \langle -\text{singular} \rangle \end{bmatrix}
\qquad\qquad
\begin{bmatrix} \langle +\text{N} \rangle \\ \langle +\text{pronoun} \rangle \\ \langle +\text{I} \rangle \\ \langle +\text{II} \rangle \\ \langle -\text{singular} \rangle \end{bmatrix}
$$

If there are two lexical entries, there should be two meanings. What are they? The sentence below might be said to a National Liberation Front envoy by a spokesman for the U. S. and South Vietnamese governments in peace negotiations:

(13)   We agree that discussion of political matters should precede discussion of military affairs.

The *we* here is ambiguous. It has at least two meanings. First, the pronoun could refer to agreement involving just the U. S. and South Vietnamese authorities. In other words it excludes the persons being addressed. Or it might be an inclusive *we*, including *you*, the persons addressed. The *we*, in

(14)   * Both we and you agree that . . .

can only be the exclusive *we*, shown as ⟨− II⟩. With the inclusive *we*, the sentence would not be acceptable.

Another set of syntactic features play an important role in the so-called article system of English. Articles are used in English to provide various kinds of semantic specificity to the nouns following them. In particular, many common nouns are either definite or indefinite; for example, *the boy* as opposed to *a boy*. The particular property possessed by the noun is reflected by the form of the article, *the* versus *a*.

(15)   The cats enjoy fried hake.

is

(16)   Cats enjoy fried hake.

The article *the* is ⟨+ definite⟩, and either singular or plural, while *a* and *an* are ⟨− definite⟩. *This, these, that,* and *those* are even more definite than *the*. They are called demonstrative articles, that is, ⟨+ demonstrative⟩. Two are ⟨+ singular⟩, the other two are ⟨− singular⟩. One more feature is needed now to distinguish *this* and *these* from *that* and *those*. The former seem to refer to something nearer, the latter to something less near. Thus, it is all right to say *this man here* or *that man there,* but not ** this man there* or ** that man here.* This property is called *nearness* or *proximity*. The features ⟨+ near⟩ and ⟨− near⟩ might reasonably be employed. Now the differences between the various articles can be expressed as follows:

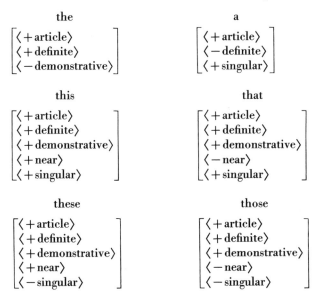

the
$$\begin{bmatrix} \langle + \text{article} \rangle \\ \langle + \text{definite} \rangle \\ \langle - \text{demonstrative} \rangle \end{bmatrix}$$

a
$$\begin{bmatrix} \langle + \text{article} \rangle \\ \langle - \text{definite} \rangle \\ \langle + \text{singular} \rangle \end{bmatrix}$$

this
$$\begin{bmatrix} \langle + \text{article} \rangle \\ \langle + \text{definite} \rangle \\ \langle + \text{demonstrative} \rangle \\ \langle + \text{near} \rangle \\ \langle + \text{singular} \rangle \end{bmatrix}$$

that
$$\begin{bmatrix} \langle + \text{article} \rangle \\ \langle + \text{definite} \rangle \\ \langle + \text{demonstrative} \rangle \\ \langle - \text{near} \rangle \\ \langle + \text{singular} \rangle \end{bmatrix}$$

these
$$\begin{bmatrix} \langle + \text{article} \rangle \\ \langle + \text{definite} \rangle \\ \langle + \text{demonstrative} \rangle \\ \langle + \text{near} \rangle \\ \langle - \text{singular} \rangle \end{bmatrix}$$

those
$$\begin{bmatrix} \langle + \text{article} \rangle \\ \langle + \text{definite} \rangle \\ \langle + \text{demonstrative} \rangle \\ \langle - \text{near} \rangle \\ \langle - \text{singular} \rangle \end{bmatrix}$$

At the more abstract deep structure level articles are not shown as separate constituents of meaning. The *definiteness* properties are *semantically* associated with *nouns*. So they are said to exist in deep structures as *features* of nouns, together with features of *person, common, concrete,* and other categories. In English a special article transformation duplicates the noun features relevant to articles to the left of the noun as a bundle of features called a *segment.* Eventually, this segment of article features is replaced by the word in the lexicon corresponding to the features in the segment. Those languages which show *definiteness* through noun suffixes would have a transformation producing a segment containing the features to the *right* of the noun and adjoining it to the noun. Ultimately, in the course of transformational derivation, the lexicon would supply an actual ending for the noun on the basis of the feature content of the segment.

The feature notation is an extremely useful way to deal with phenomena which are cross-linguistic. Not all languages have determiners, for example. But degrees of definiteness are important areas of meaning and every language has ways of expressing them. Features thus provide a useful mechanism for showing what languages have in common, and the varying rules for realizing features at the surface structure level can provide fairly precise ways of characterizing major differences between languages.

Exercises for Chapter Six

1. Using the syntactic and semantic features of nouns discussed in this chapter, work out fairly detailed lexical representations of the following nouns:
   (a) greetings
   (b) barber
   (c) Schwartz
   (d) curtain
   (e) tree
2. For each of the above, state those features, if any, which are predictable from other features and construct simplified lexical presentations wherever applicable.
3. Construct full lexical representation in terms of features for these pronouns:
   (a) I
   (b) he

    (c) she
    (d) they
    (e) it

4. Comment on the following:

    (a) The brown waves of fog toss up to me
        Twisted faces from the bottom of the street
        And tear from a passer-by with muddy skirts
        An aimless smile that hovers in the air
        And vanishes along the level of the roofs.

                                        T. S. Eliot

    (b) Surprised in this blue poise of evening
        I watch the white observatory dome that turns
        And stops, and hugely opening,
        Submits a complex eye
        To the indifference of eternity . . .

                            John Malcolm Brinnin

    (c) He turned,
        His voice splintering
        The fresh blue air
        And the soft furry minutes
        Chattered feverishly
        Then hopped back
        Behind the blankly-smiling dial.

    (d) When by now and tree by leaf
        She laughed his joy she cried his grief
        Bird by snow and stir by still
        Anyone's any was all to her.

                                e.e. cummings

    (e) Steel sings with the joy of strength
        Iron grumbles as the girders strain
        The street cars tremble on the rusty length
        And the brown rust crumbles
        In the soft-falling rain.

5. All three of these paragraphs describe the same incident. Howe, a young professor, is about to be photographed with the Dean when a particularly obnoxious student joins the two of them. Tertan, another student who does not yet know that he is to leave the college, passes by and Howe, who likes him, becomes uneasy. Compare the three paragraphs briefly. One of them was written by Lionel Trilling. Which one do you think it is? How do the syntactic differences affect the surface meaning?

(a) Tertan watched them in the incurious way people watch someone taking a photograph. Suddenly it occurred to Howe that
the boy might believe the three were posing for a picture
together. This made Howe detach himself almost rudely from
the Dean's grasp.

(b) Tertan watched them incuriously, the way people watch someone taking a photograph. Suddenly Howe detached himself
almost rudely from the Dean's grasp. He feared that the boy
would think the three were posing for a picture together.

(c) Tertan watched them in the incurious way people watch a
photograph being taken, and suddenly the thought that, to
the boy, it must seem that the three were posing for a picture
together made Howe detach himself almost rudely from the
Dean's grasp.

BIBLIOGRAPHY

JACOBS, RODERICK A. and PETER S. ROSENBAUM. *English Transformational Grammar.* Waltham, Mass.: Ginn, 1968, Chapter 12.

LAKOFF, GEORGE. "Pronouns and Reference," (mimeographed) Indiana University Linguistics Club.

McCAWLEY, JAMES D. "Where Do Noun Phrases Come From?" in Jacobs and Rosenbaum, *Readings in English Transformational Grammar.* Waltham, Mass.: Ginn, 1970.

POSTAL, PAUL M. "On So-Called 'Pronouns' in English," in Jacobs and Rosenbaum. *Readings in English Transformational Grammar.* Waltham, Mass.: Ginn, 1970.

Questions and the Representation of Meaning

7

Since feeling is first
Who pays any attention
to the syntax of things
will never wholly kiss you

e. e. cummings

In an earlier chapter we discussed simple yes–no questions and how to represent their meaning at the deep structure level. One other important type of question sentence, the WH question, has not been dealt with. Here are some WH questions:

(1) WHo drank hemlock?
(2) WHat may Napoleon buy?
(3) WHen will King Arthur return?
(4) WHere was Disraeli born?

The key constituents of the answer sentences to these questions would be noun phrases, for example:

(1a) Socrates
(2a) a ruby
(3a) December
(4a) England

But *who* is a pronoun with a ⟨+human⟩ feature and you expect a ⟨+human⟩ noun phrase in the answer; whereas *what* is ⟨−human⟩. So, a ⟨+human⟩ answer to question (2), for example, *Cleopatra*, would be a surprise. *When* differs in being a *time* word, ⟨+time⟩, and *where* has the feature ⟨+location⟩.

Deep structures for WH questions always contain a questioned noun phrase, itself containing a noun with the feature. This NP is shown with a feature $\langle +\text{WH}\rangle$ and also the feature $\langle +\text{pronoun}\rangle$. Without the $\langle +\text{WH}\rangle$ feature the NP would become a word like *someone, something, sometime, somewhere/someplace, . . .* Here is an abbreviated deep structure for the sentence:

(2)   WHat may Napoleon buy?

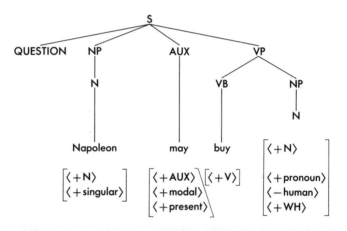

As usual, the QUESTION Transformation shifts the auxiliary around the subject noun phrase. (Irrelevant features are omitted.)

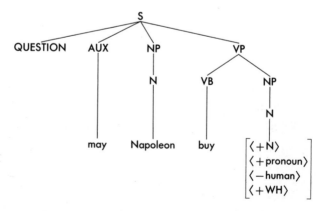

Then the WH question transformation replaces the QUESTION constituent with the noun phrase having the $\langle +\text{WH}\rangle$ feature. The latter is subsequently realized as *what:*

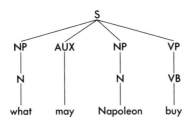

The deep structure representation of this sentence indicates with Q *I am asking you* and by the ⟨ + WH⟩ that the questioner expects to be answered with additional specifications for the NP, the additional complex of properties being represented by one or more new lexical items. If the deep structure is indeed the meaning, it might perhaps be better to replace such arbitrary symbols with *I am asking you,* and so forth.

In fact, such proposals have been made recently.[1] The native speaker normally knows when a sentence of his language is a question, a statement, or an order. When the order *Wash yourself* is given, the addressee knows that the speaker means *I order you* as part of his message. An *I* of the speaker and a *you* of the addressee is part of every message and sometimes the speaker reasserts himself in a relatively subtle way:

(5)   Joseph told me that he was going to marry that stupid little creature who lives next door to him.

Of course it is possible that Joseph said

(6)   I'm going to marry that stupid little creature who lives next door to me.

but it seems more likely that the evaluation is the speaker's contribution rather than Joseph's. The relevant part of the sentence could thus be paraphrased

(7)   . . . to marry someone who I tell you is a stupid . . .

similarly,

(8)   That idiot Snowberg is here.

---

[1] For example, John R. Ross. "On Performatives," in Jacobs and Rosenbaum. *Readings in English Transformational Grammar.* Waltham, Mass.: Ginn, 1970.

means something like *I say to you that Snowberg is here and he is an idiot.*

J. R. Ross has accumulated a number of interesting arguments for incorporating a higher sentence

$$I \begin{Bmatrix} ask \\ declare\ to \\ order \end{Bmatrix} you$$

into the underlying structure of every sentence, although the arguments are presently far from conclusive.

Exercises for Chapter Seven

1. Draw deep structure trees for the following sentences:
   (a) Who did you see?
   (b) What will console Nicodemus?
2. Show how the major transformations generate 1a and b.
3. Write lexical representations for each of the following nouns:
   (a) pencil
   (b) bushes
   (c) thumb
   (d) shrimp
   (e) Joan Baez
   (f) sickness
4. How many ways can you give basic paraphrases of this sentence of Bonamy Dobrée's?

   We feel that what is important is not
   so much truth as the way our
   minds move towards truth.

5. Describe the meaning differences you notice between Dobrée's sentence and two of your paraphrases.

BIBLIOGRAPHY

JACOBS, RODERICK A. and PETER S. ROSENBAUM. *English Transformational Grammar.* Waltham, Mass.: Ginn, 1968, Chapter 19.
———. *Introduction to Transformational Grammar: Grammar Three.* Waltham, Mass.: Ginn, 1970, Lessons 7–11.
ROSS, JOHN R. "On Performatives," in Jacobs and Rosenbaum. *Readings in English Transformational Grammar.* Waltham, Mass.: Ginn, 1970.

Simplicity and Linguistic Generalization

8

The importance of a theory lies not in the degree of
finality attained by definition and analysis, but in the
power and grasp of general principles appearing in
diverse instances.

K. J. W. Craik (1943)

The linguist who describes a language in the manner suggested by
this book does not seek merely to describe and catalog the linguistic
data. He seeks to understand the principles implicit in the linguistic
knowledge of a native speaker. Such principles allow the linguist
to express linguistic generalizations significant not only for the language described but, hopefully, for all human languages. A *grammar*
in this sense is a theory of a particular language, a theory about the
processes of the language, the significant units of the language, the
kinds of relations among these units, and other aspects of the implicit
linguistic knowledge of his language that any native speaker pos-
sesses.

One general, though not unchallenged assumption, in theory
formulation is that the more general (that is, simpler) the theory is
in regard to a given body of data, the greater the likelihood that
it will embody significant generalizations about the data. A grammar
which duplicates information in describing a particular area of syntax
is less general than one in which the information is embodied in
a single rule.

When the CLEFT SENTENCE Transformation was discussed in
Chapter Five, it was assumed that cleft sentences like the following:

(1)   What amazed Charles was the speed of the craft.
(2)   What was drunk by the guests was a strange combination of
      goat's milk and apple cider.

(3)   What the fire destroyed was the ancient Library of Alexandria.
(4)   What the film appealed to was the perfectly normal desire to sob sentimentally in the dark.
(5)   What the thunderstorm frightened was my duck-billed platypus.

were related to the corresponding non-cleft sentences below:

(6)   The speed of the craft amazed Charles.
(7)   A strange combination of goat's milk and apple cider was drunk by the guests.
(8)   The fire destroyed the ancient Library of Alexandria.
(9)   The film appealed to the perfectly normal desire to sob sentimentally in the dark.
(10)   The thunderstorm frightened my duck-billed platypus.

The considerations leading to the postulation of a single deep structure arise primarily from the basic synonymy of the pairs of sentences given. For example, the relations between the noun phrase following *was* and the verb in each cleft sentence were the same as those between the same noun phrase and the verb in the corresponding non-cleft sentence. The subject noun phrase of (7) must refer to something liquid. The following utterance would be very strange:

(11)   * The principle of gravity was drunk by the guests.

Likewise the noun phrase after *was* in (2) must be the same kind of noun phrase. The following cleft sentence is ridiculous for the same reasons as the non-cleft sentence above

(12)   * What was drunk by the guests was the principle of gravity.

Similarly the verb *frighten* in (10) requires a ⟨+ animate⟩ noun phrase as object. But the verb *frighten* in (5) also requires a ⟨+ animate⟩ noun phrase, though in this case it follows *was*. Nevertheless it is still understood as the object. Violation of this restriction produces just the same kind of semantic anomaly:

(13)   * The thunderstorm frightened the filing cabinet.
(14)   * What the thunderstorm frightened was the filing cabinet.

You might make up two rules to account for what happens to *frighten*. One could stipulate that the noun phrase following *frighten* must be ⟨+ animate⟩ in non-cleft sentences. The second could stipulate that where a cleft sentence contains *frighten*, the noun phrase after *was* (or another form of *be*) must be ⟨+ animate⟩. In fact, a third rule would be required since in passive sentences the noun phrase subject preceding *frighten* must be ⟨+ animate⟩.

(15)   * The filing cabinet was frightened by the thunderstorm.

The anomalous sentences, cleft or non-cleft, passive or active, are strange for the same reason. If synonymous cleft, non-cleft, passive, and active sentences can be related through a single deep structure, regardless of the different surface structures, then a single generalization can account for all the anomalies. The difference in position is just the result of meaning-preserving transformations. Hence, if the original deep structure is semantically anomalous because a restriction on animateness has been violated, then all surface structures derived from the deep structure must also be similarly anomalous.

If the actives and passives, or clefts and non-clefts, are regarded as not quite synonymous, then their deep structures should be alike only in the respects in which the surface sentences share common meanings. Both passive and cleft sentences show slightly different *focus* from active and non-cleft sentences respectively. Furthermore cleft sentences involve presuppositions not necessarily implied in the corresponding non-cleft sentences. Thus, as we saw before, sentences like:

What destroyed our hopes was the jailing of the dissenters.

suppose that the hearer knows that our hopes were destroyed, although he may not know what did it.

Considerations of simplicity and generality must guide linguists investigating the many shadowy areas of English syntax. They need to formulate the simplest and most general deep structures and transformations capable of explaining the phenomena. One area illustrating this rather well is that of *nominalization* (the making of sentences into noun phrases). No adequate and precise formulation is yet available, yet the general properties to be explained are quite well known now. Basically nominalization is a syntactic process relating sentence structures to nominal (or noun-like) structures synonymous with the sentence structure. For example, passages (17) and (19) use sentence structures to express semantic relationships identical or almost identical to those expressed by the passages (18) and (20) which use nominal units instead:

(17) The governor approved the law, denying that he was responsible for introducing it. This enraged the younger voters. They demanded that the law be repealed by the legislature, but that only made the legislators more obstinate.

(18) The governor's approval of the law and his denial of any responsibility for its introduction enraged the younger voters. But their demand for the repeal of the law by the legislature only made the legislators more obstinate.

(19) The waves crashed. The wind howled. The lifeboat rocked perilously. All this drove us into a state of frenzied terror.

(20) The crashing of the waves, the howling of the wind, and the perilous rocking of the lifeboat all drove us into a state of frenzied terror.

The relative stylistic merits of the passages are debatable. In general composition instructors who were asked preferred the nominalized version of the first pair and the unnominalized version of the second. But semantically both pairs of passages are interpreted similarly. The formal effects of nominalization are clear enough. The verbs *approve, deny, demand,* and *repeal,* and the adjective *responsible* were converted into noun forms: *approval, denial, demand, repeal* and *responsibility.* The original subject becomes possessive. If the verbs are transitive and no preposition appears before the object, a preposition is introduced:

(21) The governor approved the law.
(22) The governor's approval of the law . . .

Already the assumption has been made that the synonymy of the forms is not accidental but the result of a transformation process which nominalizes sentence structures. What does this assumption "buy" you? First the relation between *the governor's* and *approval* is still understood as subject and verb, although the former is not a subject and the latter is not a verb. The nominalization hypothesis provided an explanation for this. At the level of deep structure, the level where semantic interpretation takes place, both versions were in grammatical subject–verb relation. Similarly *approval* and *the law* in the nominalized form are still interpreted as if there is a verb–object relation between them. At the level of deep structure this too was present, under the nominalization hypothesis. The nominalization transformation, like any other, does not change basic semantic interpretation.

Furthermore the verb *approve* requires a ⟨+animate⟩, possibly ⟨+human⟩ subject. This is why the following sentence sounds so strange unless interpreted metaphorically:

(23)   *The oak door approved the law.

But the noun *approval* requires only a possessive noun phrase which is ⟨+animate⟩, and commonly ⟨+human⟩. Thus, what is grammatical for the sentence is grammatical for the noun phrase. What is ungrammatical for the sentence is ungrammatical for the noun phrase. The restrictions and semantic relations associated with *approval* are remarkably similar to those associated with *approve*. The nominalization hypothesis assumes that this and many parallel similarities between other pairs are not coincidences. Instead, the alternate forms are thought to be realizations of a common underlying structure, one for which only one statement of restrictions would be necessary. The general notions of nominalization are widely accepted but the precise formulation of the common deep structure is still under investigation.

Just as with cleft and passive sentences, it could be claimed that nominalized forms differ in forms and presupposition from unnominalized forms. The unnominalized sentences:

(24)   Huck admired Jim greatly. This led him to change his attitude towards a man he had once regarded as a chattel.

differ from the nominalized one

(25)   Huck's great admiration for Jim led him to change his attitude. . . .

The latter presupposes Huck's admiration whereas the former doesn't. The focus is more on the change of attitude in the second sentence. Exactly how to represent focus and presupposition is presently far from clear. But it should hopefully be clear that the transformational framework described here provides a useful basis for an investigation of meaning. It also provides a useful basis for other kinds of questions.

Some of these are psychological questions about what it is, in the area of language, that distinguishes human beings from other animals. Superficially, human beings have a mechanism for communication which other animals do not. Only human beings can learn language, which is to say that the entire human species comes into the world preprogrammed, as it were, to acquire a language when and if the correct environmental circumstances arise. A central issue in linguistics these days concerns the characteristics of this preprogramming. Just how are we preprogrammed?

The approach to this question taken by linguists has been to ask critical questions about the effects of this preprogramming. What, in other words, are we capable of doing once we know a language? Some elements of this knowledge have been enumerated in previous chapters, including such items as:

1. awareness of synonymy of utterances
2. awareness of ambiguity of utterances
3. awareness of anomaly of utterances
4. grammaticality.

From observations such as these has emerged the rudiments of a theory about the special way in which the brain of a human being works in its use of language. The brain deals with such abstract entities as deep and surface structures; it processes such structures in a fashion that can partially, at least, be described by transformational rules.

Exercises for Chapter Eight

The questions here seek to make you more aware of how to tackle linguistic problems.

1. What do you notice about the word *own* in phrases like *my own car?* What are the restrictions on the use of *own* in sentences? Consider why the following sentence may be ungrammatical:

   Although Rosinda asked her father for permission, she had no right to demolish his own car.

2. What is presupposed in the following sentences?
   (a) **The present King of France is bald.**
   (b) **When did you see the general?**

3. What do you notice in the following sentences when *Kurt* and *he* can refer to the same person? Suggest an informal rule (or two) to account for the pronoun reference phenomena.
   (a) **Kurt was sick but he refused to go to bed.**
   (b) **He was sick but Kurt refused to go to bed.**

   (c) Although Kurt was sick, he refused to go to bed.
   (d) Although he was sick, Kurt refused to go to bed.
4. Comment on the following:
   (a) Kurt was sick but the idiot wouldn't go to bed.
   (b) The idiot was sick but Kurt wouldn't go to bed.

BIBLIOGRAPHY

CHOMSKY, NOAM. *Language and Mind.* New York: Harcourt, 1968, Chapter 3.

———. "Remarks on Nominalization," in Jacobs and Rosenbaum. *Readings in English Transformational Grammar.* Waltham, Mass.: Ginn, 1970.

LANGACKER, RONALD. *"Pronominalization and the Chain of Command,"* in David Reibel and Sanford Schane. *Modern Studies in English.* Englewood Cliffs, N.J.: Prentice-Hall, 1969.

A Standard Transformational Description of the English Auxiliary

9

The study of these "auxiliary verbs" turns out to be quite crucial in the development of English grammar. We shall see that their behavior is very regular and simply describable . . .

Noam Chomsky (1957)

The school of linguistic analysis which developed the general principles for describing linguistic structure, as presented in the preceding chapters of this book, has come to be known as the *transformational* school of linguistics. And the point of view associated with this school is one which has as its central focus questions about the internalized set of abilities which make it possible for human beings to speak human languages, and to understand and produce the sentences of such languages. From this point of view, two forms of interrelated research activities become important. The first is *theoretical* and concerns the discovery and verification of universal characteristics of language, of all human languages. Included in this inventory are such items as transformations, deep structures, surface structures, features, and so forth. The second approach is *descriptive* rather than theoretical. A descriptive transformational linguist uses the framework of linguistic universals provided by the theoretical transformational linguist to describe the syntactic, semantic, and phonological properties of particular human languages, like English for example. The remainder of the book contains an informal presentation of certain interesting and revealing attempts to analyze various portions of our own language, English. Since the English auxiliary system was one of the first topics to interest transformational linguists it is an appropriate place to begin.

The *auxiliary system* is a term which refers to the syntactic behavior of a number of words and other syntactic elements which often precede and qualify in characteristic ways the semantic interpretation of the main verb of the sentence. For example, contrast the meaning of the following six sentences:

(1) Nagel eats blintzes.
(2) Nagel is eating blintzes.
(3) Nagel has eaten blintzes.
(4) Nagel has been eating blintzes.
(5) Nagel had eaten blintzes.
(6) Nagel had been eating blintzes.

In all six sentences the subject and object noun phrases remain constant, as does the stem of the main verb *eat.* However, the meaning of each of the sentences is different.

The meaning differences do seem to be related to time. Although (1) does not assign the blintz-eating event to a particular segment of time, the other sentences do. Sentence (2) concerns an ongoing present time activity; sentence (3) assigns the activity to some indefinite segment of past time. But the situation is semantically far more complex than such simple time assignments might suggest. Thus (4) is not simply a representation of (3) with an added "ongoing" emphasis. And sentences (5) and (6) are not simply (3) and (4), respectively, pushed back further into the past. They may represent activities which, in a particular discourse, occur before other activities. The adverb *already* could easily be inserted. Thus the *had* form is used in narrative primarily to relate past activities to other past activities on a relative time scale, and sometimes to relate them as "cause–effect" events. The "effect" event may be in a sentence with a *thus* or *consequently.*

(7) Nagel had been eating blintzes. Thus it was hardly surprising that he viewed the huge platter piled high with potato pancakes with a stodgy indifference amounting to distaste.

In fact, the label "ongoing present time activity" assigned to (2) is not appropriate to the formally similar (8).

(8) Nagel is leaving town.

for which the time reference could be specified by *right now, tomorrow, next year,* or even a reference to some other future event. Here, for example, it is a prediction:

(9)   Nagel is leaving town. I'm not going to let him ruin Agnew's campaign.

Faced with such an apparent morass of semantic complexity, linguists have concerned themselves more with the syntactic characteristics of such sentences — for example, which verbs (or adjectives) occur in the *be . . . ing* form and which do not:

(10)   * Mabel is knowing karate
(11)   * Mabel is being pregnant

and seeking general rules to cover the apparently complex ordering of the auxiliary elements with respect to each other.

(12)   Sigismund had been seeing Clothilde.
(13)   * Sigismund was having been seeing Clothilde
(14)   * Sigismund had being was seen Clothilde

Once a neat formulation for this had been obtained, it was easier to look at the internal ordering and attempt to relate the ordering to meaning differences. Such attempts are presently occupying some linguists.

First to deal with what traditional grammarians have labeled as *aspect.*

Sentences such as:

(15)   Mabel is arguing with the navigator.
(16)   Harry is laughing his head off.
(17)   Archibald is thinking about his navel.

are said to illustrate verb phrases in the *progressive aspect.*
Sentences like:

(18)   Mabel has taken gas.
(19)   Harry has forgotten his manners.
(20)   Archibald has fallen from a position of grace.

exemplify what grammarians called the *perfect aspect.*
And, as you might expect, the aspect of sentences like:

(21)   Mabel has been biting her nails.
(22)   Harry has been worrying about exams.
(23)   Archibald has been sleeping for hours.

is said to be *perfect progressive.*
The problem facing transformational linguists was this: Suppose

you wanted to know what kind of information the speaker of English stored in his head about English. You would have to notice that for a vast number of English verbs there exists both a non-progressive form and a progressive form (that is, with an *ing*). But are both forms of every verb actually stored in the speaker's head? Or, is there just one form, a basic form, and one rule for creating progressive forms? Linguists asking this question have concluded that speakers of English do not store *ing* forms separately, but rather generate them from non-*ing* forms when the occasion demands.

Now, how might this generative process be represented in a grammar? Imagine a deep structure in which the auxiliary carries the syntactic feature ⟨+ progressive⟩, as in the deep structure below for

(24)   Leontes is sleeping.

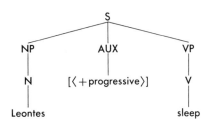

In terms of this structure it is easy to imagine a transformational process which creates verbs in their *ing* forms. Such a process, informally stated, would say the following:

> Whenever an auxiliary with the ⟨+ progressive⟩ feature precedes a real verb, add *ing* to the right of the real verb. If the main predicate element is an adjective, and therefore preceded by the copula *be*, add *ing* to the right of the *be*.

This transformational formulation thus accounts for the *ing* forms in both of the following sentences:

(25)   Leontes is slee*ping*.
(26)   Leontes is be*ing* honest.

Exactly the same kind of treatment can be applied to sentence structures with the perfect aspect, as in sentences like *John has eaten*. We posit a deep structure in which the auxiliary constituent carries the feature ⟨+ perfect⟩. Under these circumstances, the relevant transformational process would be sensitive to the existence of the ⟨+perfect⟩ feature and would add an appropriate suffix to the verb, usually either *ed* as in:

has cook*ed*
has barter*ed*

or *en* as in:

has tak*en*
has eat*en*.

Occasionally, the verb will be irregular, in which case the transformation must allow for a special form of the verb to replace the main verb, as in:

has *thought*
has *drunk*
has *left*.

The occurrence of a verb phrase with both perfect and progressive aspects provides some corroboration for the major point of this analysis, namely that the aspectual suffixes are added transformationally to the right-hand side of the constituent, which itself is to the right of a primary aspect constituent. Suppose you have a deep structure wherein the auxiliary was marked with the features ⟨+perfect⟩ and ⟨+progressive⟩, as would be required for a sentence like:

(27)   Balthazar has been worrying.

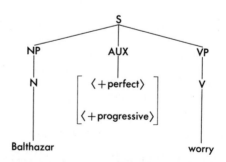

The first transformation to apply to this structure would separate out perfect and progressive as constituents by producing an independent progressive constituent, as in:

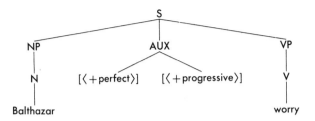

Ultimately the perfect segment will end up as the appropriate form of *have* — that is, *has;* the progressive segment will end up as *be.* However, notice what the effect of the aspectual transformation will be. The suffix *en* will be moved to the right of the progressive segment and the suffix *ing* will be moved to the right of the main verb *worry,* giving, finally:

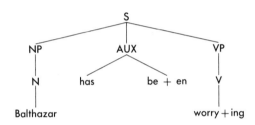

The term *auxiliary* in the discussion of many linguistic phenomena is more a cover term for a class of events which go on between certain elements of sentences than it is the name of a particular constituent structure. In this discussion of aspect in English, the term *auxiliary* has been used to refer to the special class of verbal elements preceding main verbs.

Such elements include words like *can, may, will,* and *shall* — usually termed *modal auxiliaries* — and their so-called "past" forms: *could, might, would,* and *should,* and also a variety of forms like *be about to, be going to, be able to, ought to, must,* and *need (not).* Where these occur in the auxiliary, they always precede the aspect elements. Some are ordered with respect to each other:

(28)   Cleo is going to be able to appear on Friday.
(29)   * Cleo is able to be going to appear on Friday
(30)   * Cleo is able to ought to appear on Friday

while others are mutually exclusive:

(31)   * Cleo must ought to appear on Friday
(32)   * Cleo ought to must appear on Friday

The modals *must* and *ought to* appear to be semantically contradictory. The first suggests some kind of outside compulsion; the other suggests an inner sense of moral obligation. If, in (32), the *must* is replaced by the partially synonymous *be obliged to*, the result is grammatical:

(33)   Cleo ought to be obliged to appear on Friday.

But note that the semantic relation between *Cleo* and *ought to* has changed. The semantic subject of *ought* is now the unspecified semantic subject of *be obliged to*. Thus (33) has the fairly close paraphrase:

(34)   Someone ought to oblige Cleo to appear on Friday.

An analysis like the one presented is thus only an important first step to a more thorough semantically-based analysis.

Some important conclusions can be reached with little appeal to the semantic criteria. For example, it appears to be a purely formal fact that only the first auxiliary word shifts around the subject when a yes–no question is formed:

(35)   Will Jupiter be seeing Minerva tomorrow?
(36)   * Will be Jupiter seeing Minerva tomorrow?
(37)   * Likes Jupiter Minerva?

Sentence (37) shows that only an auxiliary word can be shifted. If the deep structure contains no auxiliary word, the special auxiliary *do* is introduced and takes on the tense and number specifications that would otherwise be carried by the verb.

(38)   * Jupiter does like Minerva.[1]

Then the regular question transformation applies:

(39)   Does Jupiter like Minerva?

Yet the description of the auxiliary presented here provides a very reasonable account of the workings of the auxiliary, though not an explanation. This account would not have been possible without the discovery of how transformational processes work in languages. It

---

[1] As a surface structure, (38) is grammatical only if "does" has emphatic stress.

is worthwhile to understand why this is so. If you don't assume that transformations play a role in human language, you would have to conclude that a speaker of English learns the *perfect* form (that is, the *ing* form) of verbs by being exposed to and memorizing all of these forms.

But this hypothesis is absurd. Have you, for example, ever met any native speaker of English over seven who, knowing the non-progressive form of a verb, did not know correctly whether or not it had a progressive form and what that progressive form was? Or, if we present you with the verb *urglitemporize* and tell you that it means *to flounder under a sea of paperwork*, you know, without having heard the word before, that it will have a progressive form *urglitemporizing*.

Knowing English, in this case, means knowing the transformations of English and, as a consequence, knowing the progressive forms of verbs that you have never heard before. The standard model of transformational grammar was able to capture such insights. But more recently, transformational linguists have sought to go further and account for other crucial native speaker knowledge. One such treatment is described in the next chapter.

Exercises for Chapter Nine

1. Using tree diagrams in the same way as in the chapter, explain how the following sentences are generated:
   (a) Lobbyists were obstructing legislation.
   (b) Sophia has fainted.
   (c) Kimba had been fighting panthers.
2. In what ways do the modal auxiliaries *can, may, will,* and *shall* differ from verbs?
3. From the negative and interrogative sentences corresponding to the sentences below, what inferences can you draw as to the role of the auxiliary *do?*
   (a) The grape-picker understands Spanish and English.
   (b) Solomon inspected the temple last Friday.
4. In the following sentences the auxiliaries cause the sentences to be ambiguous. Describe the ambiguities.
   (a) Judith may leave tomorrow.
   (b) Goliath can remove that tree trunk.

5. Explain the various meanings you understand in the following sentences:
   (a) May Glenda go on the factory outing?
   (b) Might Glenda go on the factory outing?

6. Give three or four ways in which *may* differs from *might* in other contexts than 5a and 5b.

BIBLIOGRAPHY

CHOMSKY, NOAM. *Syntactic Structures.* S-Gravenhage: Mouton, 1957, pp. 15–17, 38–40, 61–68.

JACOBS, RODERICK A. and PETER S. ROSENBAUM. *English Transformational Grammar.* Waltham, Mass.: Ginn, 1968, Chapters 14, 15, and 16.

TWADDELL, W. FREEMAN. *The English Verb Auxiliaries.* Providence: Brown University Press, 1960.

A More Semantically-Based Transformational Description of the English Auxiliary

10

. . . we will have a neater analysis of contemporary English . . . if we recognize no modal auxiliaries at all. We will then have to say of such a verb as "can" that it is a transitive whose complement must be infinitival . . .

Ralph B. Long (1961)

The description of the English auxiliary in the last chapter is far from complete, of course. But it does give a fair idea of how the problems have been tackled. The discussion in this chapter is also incomplete but the problems are tackled in a slightly different way. The discussion here treats deep structure as being the basic meaning level — a more abstract semantically-oriented level than that assumed in Chapter Nine. Consequently, deep structures look less like surface structures than did the deep structures of the previous chapter.

From this viewpoint, the description of the auxiliary in the preceding chapter is inadequate because it fails to specify important linguistic information that the native speaker is aware of, information that should be important to a grammatical description of English. For example, the sentence:

(1) Eric John should climb Mt. Kanchenjunga.

indicates that Eric John has, in the opinion of the speaker, some kind of obligation with respect to the climbing. But it also indicates that Eric John is the one to do the climbing. *Eric John* is semantically the subject both of *should* and of *climb*. The sentence is assigned a deep structure equivalent to the following rough paraphrase:

(2)   * Eric John should do something namely Eric John climb Mt. Kanchenjunga

which could be shown this way:

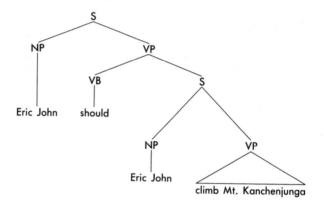

The auxiliary here has been treated as a main verb with the remainder of the sentence as the object of *should.* The deletion of the second *Eric John* is done by the Identical Noun Phrase Deletion rule described in an earlier chapter. The verb *should* differs from *ought* in not requiring the *to* complementizer before the verb of the embedded sentence. This kind of description shows that the identity of form of the *to* complementizer in sentences like:

(3)   I allowed Eric John *to* climb Mt. Kanchenjunga.

to the *to* in

(4)   Eric John ought *to* climb Mt. Kanchenjunga.

is not a coincidence but a manifestation of the same embedded sentence phenomenon.

One major surface difference between auxiliaries and main verbs is that only the latter are fully inflected, that is, take *-s* in the third person present or take the progressive *be . . . ing* form. In one sense, then, the argument may seem to be about nothing. Auxiliaries are a special subclass of verbs. While this may be adequate at the surface level, such a distinction cannot be maintained at the deep structure level, the level of meaning, as the following basically synonymous pairs should suggest:

(5) He can do only four press-ups.
(6) He is able to do only four press-ups.

(7) He dare not try any more.
(8) He doesn't dare try any more.

Treating the auxiliary as a main verb in deep structure allows sentences like the following:

(9)   Joseph won't budge.
(10) Joseph refuses to budge.
(11) Joseph doesn't want to budge.

to be treated in the same way at the deep structure level. The verb *budge* has, at this semantically significant level, the subject noun phrase *Joseph* which is deleted by a later transformation. The verb *will* (like the verbs *try* and *be*) requires the lower sentence subject to be identical to its own subject.

Such a treatment takes all the auxiliaries to be main verbs in deep structure. Thus, the *be* part of the progressive aspect *be . . . ing* is also treated as a main verb. The sentence

(12) You were carving a statue.

has this deep structure analysis:

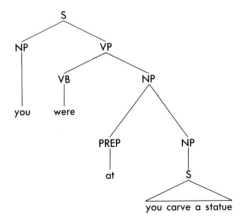

The complementizer *ing* goes onto *carve* and the second *you* is deleted under identity, along with the *at*. Just as the *for* part of the *for . . . to* complementizer is retained in some current dialects and also in old ones:

> . . . for to catch a whale.

so the *at* or the abbreviated *a-*:

(13)   You were at carving a statue.
(14)   You were a-carvin' a statue.

Since the embedded sentence is a noun phrase complement, it can be pronominalized as *it,* in which case the *at* is retained in almost all dialects. Thus the structure underlying

(15)   You were carving a statue when I entered and you were still carving a statue when I left.

can be transformed so as to end up:

(16)   You were carving a statue when I entered and you were still at it when I left.

Imagine a situation in which someone has been detaining two brothers against their will. After a silent decision to release them, he could say:

(17)   I permit the brothers to return home today.

The speaker gives the permission — *I* is the subject of *permit.* The permission is given to the brothers — *the brothers* is the object of *permit,* and *the brothers* are the ones to return home — *the brothers* is the semantic subject of *return home.* A deep structure representation could show these facts as follows:

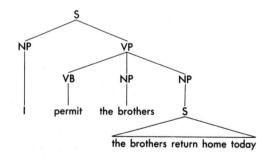

This has also a nominalized form

(18)   My permission to the brothers for the brothers to return home today . . .

which is reduced by identity deletion to either

(19)   My permission to the brothers to return home today . . .

or

(20)   My permission for the brothers to return home today . . .

But one other alternative to

(17)   I permit the brothers to return home today.

is the very different looking

(21)   The brothers may return home today.

The two sentences are basically synonymous. Sentence (21) contains the notion that the speaker is conveying permission, that the permission is being conveyed to the brothers and that the brothers are the ones to leave. Yet the surface structure of the sentence is quite distinct. The empowering or permission-granting word is *may* rather than *permit* and the speaker is not represented by an *I*. Although the *may* has *the brothers* as its surface subject, a more abstract deep structure treats *may* as a verb like *permit* and includes the *I* as its semantic subject. The deep structure is consequently very much like that for (17). Here are both of them:

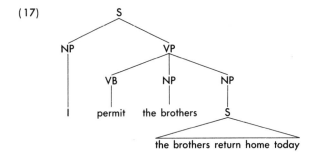

(21)

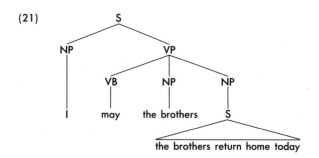

The likeness of the deep structures reflects the semantic interpretation common to the two surface structures. The difference in surface forms comes about by the application of different transformations to the sentences. Transformations delete the *I* and the second mention of *the brothers.* By a regular transformation the noun phrase *the brothers,* which is the one immediately to the right of the verb, is shifted to the empty initial position, yielding sentence (21).[1]

Here is a very different deep structure, the approximate one underlying

(22)   It may be that the brothers return home today.

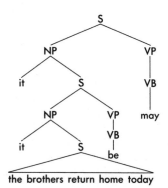

---

[1] Some recent semantically-based transformational grammars have assumed that English has a very different basic order in deep structure. Though the normal surface order is Subject–Verb–Object (SVO), the underlying order is Verb–Subject–Object (VSO). There are many good reasons for this — which cannot be gone into here. Such an ordering either simplifies or makes unnecessary a number of transformations. The subject shift transformation

The EXTRAPOSITION Transformation shifts the lowest sentence to the position after *be:*

it [it be the brothers return home today] may

Then the same transformation applies to the whole sentence, yielding:

it may it be the brothers return home today.

After deletion of the second *it* and insertion of the complementizer *that,* the sentence (22) is generated. But an alternative surface form can also be generated. By another transformation the subject of the lowest sentence becomes the subject of the highest sentence. This transformation, known as SUBJECT RAISING, is, as you will see in later chapters, an important and quite general one. PREDICATE RAISING shifts the predicate *return home today* to the end of the highest verb phrase. The verb *be* is deleted. The result is the sentence:

(23)   The brothers may return home today.

which has the same meaning as

(22)   It may be that the brothers return home today.

that is, it arises from the same deep structure. But another interesting and important fact is that it is identical in form with (21).

Thus this analysis shows that the sentence

(21)   The brothers may return home today.
(23)   The brothers may return home today.

is ambiguous because it arises from two distinct deep structures. The transformations happen to relate the different meanings to a single form.

The main verb analysis of auxiliaries is thus a useful one, though much more work has to be done to establish it. It makes superficially simple sentences like

(24)   Hemingway must have been pretending.

---

referred to in the text is a general one needed to generate passive sentences, sentences with the expletive "there," and many other types of sentence. See James D. McCawley, "English as a VSO Language," *Language* (June 1970), for further details.

seem quite complex even at the surface level after the various transformations, such as deletion, have been applied:

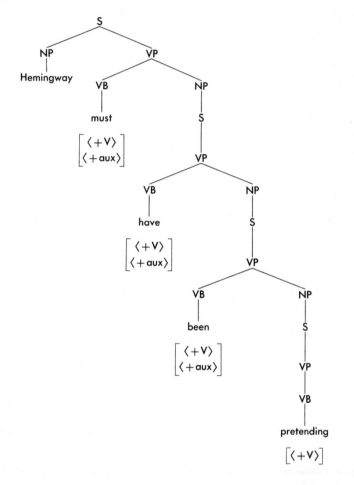

The auxiliary verbs have the feature ⟨+aux⟩ to show their unique
characteristics of lack of inflection and inversion in question sentences.

The tree above shows each auxiliary verb as a separate constituent.
Since deletion transformations should only be able to delete constituents, the following predicate constituents should be deletable:

(a) pretending
(b) been pretending

(c) have been pretending
(d) must have been pretending

while these non-constituents should not

(e) have been
(f) must have been

The sentence

(25)   Lewis must have been pretending and Hemingway must have
        been pretending too

can have the (a) constituent deleted:

(26)   Lewis must have been pretending and Hemingway must have
        been too

or (b):

(27)   Lewis must have been pretending and Hemingway must have
        too

or (c):

(28)   Lewis must have been pretending and Hemingway must too

or (d):

(29)   Lewis must have been pretending and Hemingway too.

But deletion of the non-constituents (e) and (f) result in non-sentences:

(30)   * Lewis must have been pretending and Hemingway must
        pretending too
(31)   * Lewis must have been pretending and Hemingway pretending
        too

Such syntactic evidence supports the arguments for a more abstract "semantic" deep structure.

Exercises for Chapter Ten

1. Draw deep structure trees for the following, after the manner of
   this chapter:
   (a) Humphrey was courting Elvira.
   (b) Jack can beat Fitzgerald tonight. [choose the interpretation
       that's more obvious to you]

2. Explain how these deep structures become surface structures.
3. Compare and contrast Chapters Nine and Ten with the much fuller traditional treatment in R. B. Long, *The Sentence and Its Parts.*
4. In a novel, short story, or serious article, find a short paragraph containing several auxiliary verbs. Discuss their meanings in the paragraph.

BIBLIOGRAPHY

JACOBS, RODERICK A. "Recent Developments in Transformational Grammar," *The English Record* (April 1969), pp. 52–59.

LONG, RALPH. *The Sentence and Its Parts.* Chicago: University of Chicago Press, 1961, pp. 122–151.

McCAWLEY, JAMES. "Tense and Time Reference in English," in C. J. Fillmore and D. T. Langendoen. *Proceedings of the First Ohio State Conference on Semantics.* New York: Holt (forthcoming).

——. "English as a VSO Language," *Language* (1970), *46*, 2, pp. 286–299.

ROSS, JOHN R. "Auxiliaries as Main Verbs," M.I.T. (unpublished mimeograph, 1968, obtainable from Indiana University Linguistic Club).

——. "Capping and the Order of Constituents," in *Proceedings of the Tenth International Congress of Linguists.* Bucharest, (forthcoming).

Verb Phrases and Verbals

11

In describing English verbs, I am going to distinguish a
countable set of parts, and discern a countable set of relations. And the shocking aspect of it is that I am going
to say — sometimes state and always imply — that when
that has been done there will be nothing left.

Martin Joos (1964)

In the early days of transformational grammar verb phrases were
regarded as comparatively simple constituents not too different at the
deep structure level from their surface structure form. As you should
have seen from the previous chapter, such a simplistic solution is
no longer feasible. Take for example the following pairs of sentences:

(1) It appears that Jeremy dislikes garlic.
(2) Jeremy appears to dislike garlic.

(3) It turned out that Jeremy was talented.
(4) Jeremy turned out to be talented.

There are a number of reasons to believe that both pairs of sentences
have underlying structures in common. First, the pairs are completely synonymous. Secondly, they share the same set of semantic
restrictions. In the same way that the sentence

(5) * It appears that garlic likes Jeremy.

is anomalous, so too is the sentence

(6) * Garlic appears to dislike Jeremy.

For such reasons, it has been suggested that both sentences have
the same deep structure, by some even that sentences (3) and (4)

are produced through a transformational rule which acts on some form of sentences (1) and (2).

Similar claims can be and have been made for the transformational derivation of a certain number of sentence types containing modals. For example, *may* and *could* in such sentences as

(7)   O'Casey may dislike drama.
(8)   O'Casey could come next Tuesday if we are not careful.

are closely related to the meanings of the same two words in

(9)   It may be that O'Casey dislikes drama.
(10)   It could be that O'Casey will come next Tuesday if we are not careful.

Of course not all such verbs and modals have *it* variants as surface structures, and it is equally true that the surface variants, though basically synonymous, are not exact paraphrases. The modal *must* has a number of interpretations. Under one of them, both sentence structures are possible:

(11)   Napoleon must be sick.
(12)   It must be that Napoleon is sick.

But the "compulsion" *must* allows only one form:

(13)   Napoleon must come immediately.
(14)   * It must be that Napoleon comes immediately.

although the latter may have been grammatical in earlier forms of English.

In our present state of knowledge, claims about the generation of such pairs are still quite speculative. But, as the previous chapter showed, they do suggest interesting possibilities for explaining a whole range of phenomena never successfully accounted for. For instance, *become* may originate in an upper sentence, not of course as the actual physical word *become* but as a complex set of features which might also be realized as *come to be* or *come about*. So the structure underlying the old-fashioned-sounding sentence (15):

(15)   It came $\begin{Bmatrix} \text{to be} \\ \text{about} \end{Bmatrix}$ that the soup was thick.

is related to:

(16)   The soup became thick.

possible through transformations like IT REPLACEMENT or, in a more recent formulation, subject and predicate raising. But there is another interesting consequence. The set of features which underlie *come to be, become, turn, grow,* and *come about* in their related sentences may also be realized as a verbal suffix *en.* So, besides sentences (15) and (16) above, there is also sentence (17):

(17)   The soup thickened.

Verbal elements possessing this underlying set of features representing change of state, that is, from thin to thick, have been called *inchoative.* Whatever the surface forms, this inchoative element is very much a part of the semantic interpretation. The verbal *thicken* has the meaning of *thick* together with the notion of change of state called inchoative.

Curiously, all variants are not possible for other adjectives. They are fine for

(18)   It came about that her cheeks were red.
(19)   Her cheeks came to be red.
(20)   Her cheeks became red.
(21)   Her cheeks reddened.

and for *black, hard, soft, tight, deep,* but not for *green, stern, atrocious, literate.*

(22)   It came about that the leaves were green.
(23)   The plants came to be green.
(24)   The plants became green.
(25)   * The plants $\left\{ \begin{array}{l} \text{greened} \\ \text{greenened} \end{array} \right\}$.

Suppose, as some linguists do, that there was an even higher sentence with another "deep" verb, this time one with a causation interpretation. So a structure something like:

(26)   * Sebastian $\left\{ \begin{array}{l} \text{brought it about} \\ \text{caused it} \end{array} \right\}$ that it came to be that the soup was thick.

could become:

(27)   Sebastian brought it about that the soup $\left\{ \begin{array}{l} \text{became} \\ \text{came to be} \end{array} \right\}$ thick.

or, more interestingly,

(28)   Sebastian brought it about that the soup thickened.

This hypothetical structure would explain the fact that even if the *bring it about* verb is not realized as a physical element in the surface structure, it is still possible to retain the causative meaning by shifting the subject of *thickened* to the object position, and using the causer as the subject noun phrase:

(29)   Sebastian thickened the soup.

Note that in the sentence above *thickened* has a causative meaning lacking in:

(30)   The soup thickened.

Any word that can take on an inchoative verbal form can also take on a causative verbal form, though the converse isn't true, for example,

(31)   Karloff frightened the boy.
(32)   * The boy frightened.

This analysis accounts for apparently disparate phenomena and also for the ways native speakers interpret such sentences.

Such an analysis can be extended even further, however, so that *dead*, for example, becomes, with a higher inchoative verb, *die* and then with a higher causative verb *kill*. This provides an explanation for the interpretation of *kill* as *cause to be dead*, and *die* as *become dead*. To take another example, the sentence:

(33)   Ignatius married Clarissa.

has two meanings. One is associated with the simple meaning, which is, roughly, *be in the state of matrimony*. The other contains an underlying causative and means something like *caused Clarissa to be in the state of matrimony*, that is, Ignatius performed the wedding ceremony.

Analyses like this[1] are based upon interpreting deep structures

---

[1] For further discussion, see, for example, G. Lakoff, *On the Nature of Syntactic Irregularity*, Report No. NSF-16, The Computation Laboratory of Harvard University, 1965; J. Gruber, *Functions of the Lexicon in Formal Descriptive Grammars*, System Development Corporation, Santa Monica, 1967; R. A. Jacobs and P. S. Rosenbaum, *Readings in English Transformational Grammar*, Ginn, 1970. Much of this chapter is based on these sources and also on our more advanced book, *English Transformational Grammar*, Ginn, 1968.

as basically representations of meaning relationships. At present much more investigation is required before such analyses can be accepted without qualms. They are interesting because they are firmly based upon linguistic data and make a genuine attempt to explicate the native speaker's intuitions about form and meaning. They further hold promise of a universal semantic base for the grammars of all languages, a goal dreamed of by the universal grammarians of the seventeenth and eighteenth centuries but one which never became even remotely attainable until the development of transformational grammar.

The formulation of a universal base of deep structure for all human languages presents many, many difficulties. For example, some languages such as Chinese make no distinction between verbs and adjectives. In Malay, Indonesian, and the American Indian languages of the Yuman family the distinction is slight. But in English, verbs and adjectives appear to be distinct classes. How can these diverse languages have common deep structures?

Semantic criteria are not too helpful here since some languages use adjectives where English might employ verbs, or vice versa. For example:

(34)   He is tall.

might in another language be expressed something like this:

(35)   * He talls

This suggests that adjectives and verbs are more closely related that it might seem. Even in English, you can use an adjective, as in:

(36)   He is hungry for fame.

or you can use the verb form:

(37)   He hungers for fame.

Both require the same preposition, and both require an animate subject, $\langle +$ animate$\rangle$ in feature notation. It makes sense to suggest that the two sentences share deep structures which have a great deal in common. If they are not quite synonymous, at least their deep structures must correspond to the extent that they share roughly the same interpretation. Verbs and adjectives do differ syntactically. Verb forms have their tense incorporated into them, for example, *walks, walked,* whereas adjectives cannot: * *talls,* * *talled.*

Instead tense is incorporated into the copula *be* preceding the adjectives: *is tall, was tall.* If both verbs and adjectives were said to share a verbal feature, say ⟨+VB⟩, the differences should also be represented as a feature, say ⟨+V⟩ for verbs and ⟨−V⟩ for adjectives.

Two important verb groups are the action ⟨+action⟩, and non-action, ⟨−action⟩ verbs. Action verbs like *jump, teach, drive,* can occur in regular imperatives:

(38)   Jump over that fence!
(39)   Teach Louis to write sonnets!
(40)   Drive your wife insane!

They may occur in embedded sentences like:

(41)   Cyrus persuaded her to jump over that fence.
(42)   Rosina persuaded Clarence to teach Louis to write sonnets.
(43)   Mrs. Godwin persuaded Percy to drive his wife insane.

Finally ⟨+action⟩ verbs may occur with progressive aspect, for example,

(44)   She is jumping over that fence.
(45)   Clarence is teaching Louis to write sonnets.
(46)   Percy is driving his wife insane.

But none of this is true for non-action verbs, verbs like *resemble, know, own.* Imperatives don't work too well at all:

(47)   * Resemble my father!
(48)   * Know what Bridey Murphy did!
(49)   * Own Manhattan Island.

In embedded sentences, these ⟨−action⟩ verbs sound equally strange:

(50)   * Mao persuaded Gina Lollobrigida to resemble my father.
(51)   * Buckley persuaded Rogers to know what Bridey Murphy did.
(52)   * Ricky persuaded Peter to own Manhattan Island.

With progressive aspect, these ⟨−action⟩ verbs render the sentences ungrammatical:

(53)   * Gina is resembling my father.
(54)   * Rogers is knowing what Bridey Murphy did.
(55)   * Peter is owning Manhattan Island.

Now, if the same ⟨+action⟩ and ⟨−action⟩ categories were to be found in adjectives also, this would provide further grounds for grouping together verbs and adjectives as verbals. In fact, there are two such groups. Adjectives like *careful, honest, patient* are ⟨+action⟩:

(56) Imperative Sentence: Be careful!
(57) Embedded Sentence: Edgar persuaded Dick to be careful.
(58) Progressive Sentence: Dick is being very careful.

But adjectives like swarthy, pregnant, purple, are ⟨−action⟩.

There is other evidence of the common characteristics of verbs and adjectives. Some verbs like *keep* are transitive (that is, have an object noun phrase), while others, like *elapse,* are intransitive. But note that some adjectives are in some sense also transitive, that is, have an object noun phrase, although a preposition must also appear:

(59) His father is fond of artichokes.

but not

(60) * His father is fond.

On the other hand, *swarthy* and *infinite* are intransitive:

(61) His father is swarthy.

but not

(62) * His father is swarthy of chickenpox.

Like verbs, adjectives may be either transitive or intransitive.

The case for considering adjectives and verbs together as verbals seems strong. Processes like nominalization affect verbals, regardless of whether they are adjectives or verbs; for example, these sentences:

(63) He is *able* to run the mile in three minutes.
(64) He *admired* Bannister.

may be nominalized as:

(65) His *ability* to run the mile in three minutes . . .
(66) His *admiration* for Bannister . . .

But what of one other primary difference — the presence of the copula *be* before adjectives in the predicate but not before verbs? Not very crucial. In many languages, Russian or Indonesian, for example, there is no copula *be*. It is possible that *be* is not a deep structure phenomenon at all. English, it is supposed, simply has a COPULA Transformation which introduces the copula before a verbal which is ⟨−V⟩, that is, an adjective. Thus, deep structures with verbs will look more like deep structures with adjectives. Here are hypothetical deep structure trees for:

(67) Wittgenstein pondered.
(68) Wittgenstein was thoughtful.

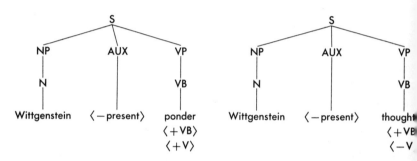

Since the tree on the right contains a verbal which is ⟨−V⟩, the copula *be* will be transformationally introduced[2] and the past tense feature will be incorporated into it.

The view that verbs and adjectives are both verbals is an attractive one which accounts for many phenomena. Nevertheless it should still be regarded as a hypothesis rather than a proven fact. Some of the same kinds of arguments can be used to show that nouns and verbals should also belong to the same deep structure class:

(69) Be a hero! (70) * Be a pterodactyl!
(71) We persuaded him to be a hero. (72) * We persuaded him to be a pterodactyl.
(73) He is being a hero. (74) * He is being a pterodactyl.

This might suggest that forms in the lexicon are not specified as nouns or verbals for most words. Once the forms are introduced into deep structures they take on the class characteristics of the tree branch

---

[2] One other possibility is to follow the example of Chapter Ten and treat *be* as a higher verb, one always in the deep structure for adjectives. But here a problem arises concerning universals. Are copula verbs like *be* to be postulated even for languages that lack them in surface structure?

on which they appear. Thus the notion 〈attract〉 in the lexicon might become *attract* or *attractive* in some positions and *attraction* in others. So far too little work has been done on this to justify any firm conclusions.

However the fact is that speakers of English detect basic semantic similarity in sentences containing verbal elements which are, on the surface, quite different syntactically. The problem posed for linguistic research is to gain some understanding of just what it is that such sentences share, what it is that can explain the intuitions that English speakers have about such sentences.

Exercises for Chapter Eleven

1. In your own words, present at least two arguments supporting the hypothesis that the two sentences below are transformationally related to roughly the same deep structure:
   (a) It seems that soggy pecans crack rather easily.
   (b) Soggy pecans seem to crack rather easily.
2. Assume that sentence (b) above is derived from the structure underlying sentence (a). Construct an abbreviated deep structure for sentence (a). Treat *soggy pecans* simply as an NP and *rather easily* as an adverbial phrase ADV.
3. List the alterations that would have to be made to the tree you have just created if this tree were to be transformed into the surface structure tree for sentence (b).
4. Adjectives and verbs have many quasi-semantic properties in common, thus leading many linguists to suspect that the distinction between verbs and adjectives is more a surface structure than a deep structure phenomenon. This view is supported by the fact that the categories *verb* and *adjective* are not universal, both appearing in all human languages. In terms of semantic properties discussed in this chapter and any others you may think of, separate the following verbs and adjectives into two groups, each containing noun verbs and noun adjectives. Justify your grouping according to semantic or syntactic considerations.
   (a) wet; (b) tasty; (c) sing; (d) own; (e) brave; (f) reveal; (g) persuade; (h) equal; (i) identical; (j) prudent; (k) look; (l) exist.
5. Like verbs, adjectives may either be transitive or intransitive. Create a list of transitive adjectives containing six items. Be sure to give example sentences for each adjective.
6. If verbs and adjectives have a common underlying structure, it

becomes necessary to explain one very important surface structure difference. State this difference and, in your own words, explain how this difference might come about in terms of transformational rules.

BIBLIOGRAPHY

GRUBER, J. *Functions of the Lexicon in Formal Descriptive Grammars.* Santa Monica: System Development Corporation, 1967.

JACOBS, RODERICK A. "Syntax and Meaning," *English Record,* (April 1970).

JACOBS, RODERICK A. and PETER S. ROSENBAUM. *English Transformational Grammar.* Waltham, Mass.: Ginn, 1968, Chapters 8 and 9, pp. 63–66; Chapters 13 and 27.

JACOBS, RODERICK A. and PETER S. ROSENBAUM. *Readings in English Transformational Grammar.* Waltham, Mass.: Ginn, 1970, Papers by C. Fillmore, R. B. Lees, N. Chomsky, and G. Lakoff.

LAKOFF, GEORGE. *Syntactic Irregularity.* New York: Holt, forthcoming.

Restrictive Relative Clauses

12

There is another Particular in our Language which is a
great Instance of our Frugality of Words, and that is the
suppressing of several Particles, which must be produced
in other Tongues to make a Sentence intelligible: This
often perplexes the best Writers, when they find the Relatives, *Who, which,* or *that,* at their Mercy whether it
may have Admission or not.

Joseph Addison (1711)

It is not hard to understand why grammarians are interested in
relative clauses. Since grammarians are trying to understand how
speakers can construct and understand new sentences, relative
clauses — which provide ways of referring to an infinite number of
entities — are extremely relevant.

A relative clause provides a way of making reference to an infinite
number of entities without taxing a speaker's memory. When you
say "the book on the table," you are referring to a specific object
for which an English word exists. You could invent one: "Hand
me the glurch!" meaning "Hand me the book on the table!" In
a sense the noun phrase *the book* itself is understood as a kind of
relative like *the thing which is a book.* But if there were a special
word for *the book on the table,* another for *the book on the refrig-
erator,* and so on, there would have to be billions of extra words
to remember since there are billions of places for a book to be.
Instead you use a sentence telling where the book is and you embed
it as a relative clause right after *the book.* This way it is quite clear
that you are referring to a particular book.

How are relative clauses formed, and what are the meaning relationships both within them and also between the relative clause and

the parts of the sentence containing the relative clause? First look at the following sentences:

(1)   *The devil* seized the children.
(2)   *Proserpine* opened the gates.

You know that the noun phrases *the devil* and *Proserpine* are subject noun phrases. They are permuted, characteristically, by the passive transformation:

(3)   The children were seized by *the devil.*
(4)   The gates were opened by *Proserpine.*

The following strings of words, however, are not sentences:

(5)   who(m) the devil seized
(6)   which Proserpine opened

Still, the native speaker perceives the same kinds of basic relationships in these segments. The noun phrases *the devil* and *Proserpine* are still considered subject noun phrases. The object noun phrases in the verb phrases containing *seized* and *opened* seem to be *who(m)* or *which*. Use of the optional suffix *m* for *who* confirms that this relative pronoun is in fact the object noun phrase. Indeed, these relative clauses have passive equivalents:

(7)   who were seized by the devil
(8)   which were opened by Proserpine

The question now is what *who* and *which*, called relative pronouns, actually *mean* when they occur as object noun phrases in

(9)   who(m) the devil seized
(10)   which Proserpine opened

Another way to ask this question is to ask how they should be represented in the deep structure. To begin the inquiry, you know that *who(m)* normally refers to something human and *which* to something non-human. Furthermore, in the sentences

(11)   The children who(m) the devil seized tormented Don Juan.
(12)   The gates which Proserpine opened overlooked the river.

who(m) obviously means *the children* and *which* means *the gates.* In other words the relative pronouns *who(m)* and *which* have actually replaced entire noun phrases. The deep structure of the first sentence could be roughly represented this way:

(1)

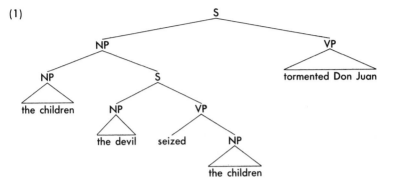

When a noun phrase, such as *the children* in the upper sentence of the diagram, is identical to some noun phrase in the lower sentence, the RELATIVE CLAUSE Transformation first converts the article of the second noun phrase into a WH word or *that*. *Who* and *which* are WH words and choice between them depends on whether the noun is human or not. The noun phrase has now been relativized. Next, if the noun phrase does not already begin the lower sentence it is shifted to the beginning.

So the first part of the RELATIVE CLAUSE Transformation actually yields something like the following:

(13) ⇒ the children who children the devil seized tormented Don Juan
(14) ⇒ the gates which gates Proserpine opened overlooked the river.

There is some historical evidence supporting this formulation. In earlier days, when *which* could be used like *that*, for either human or non-human noun phrases, no other changes would have been necessary other than the substitution of *which* for the article in the noun phrase to be relativized:

(15) The children which children the devil seized tormented Don Juan.
(16) The gates which gates Proserpine opened overlooked the river.

This older construction still survives in legal jargon. Today, in everyday English, the noun following *who* or *which* is normally deleted:

(11)   The children who the devil seized tormented Don Juan.
(12)   The gates which Proserpine opened overlooked the river.

In sum then, the RELATIVE CLAUSE Transformation first sub-stitutes *who, which,* or *that* for the determiner (or article) of the identical NP in the relative clause sentence. Then the *relativized* noun phrase is brought to the front of the relative clause sentence, if it is not already there. Finally, the relativized noun is dropped. So when the *subject* of the relative clause sentence is itself the identical one, it is not moved, since it already heads the sentence.

(2)

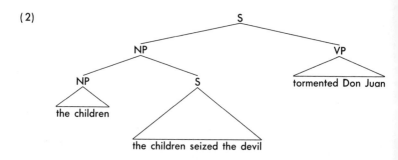

(17)   ⇒ The children who seized the devil tormented Don Juan.

Similarly if you had passivized the relative clause sentence of diagram (1) before applying the RELATIVE CLAUSE Transformation, that is,

(18)   the children the children were seized by the devil tormented Don Juan

the identical noun phrase would be in the front of the lower sentence. The relative clause transformation would simply convert the article into *who* (or *that*) and delete the noun:

(19)   The children who were seized by the devil tormented Don Juan.

What remains to be explained is how the sentence just above is related to the synonymous sentence

(20)   The children seized by the devil tormented Don Juan.

The relative pronoun *who* and the copula *were* are not always needed in the surface structure. In fact, they may be deleted by a transformation called RELATIVE CLAUSE REDUCTION.[1] This converts the structures of

(21) The unicorn which was in the garden bothered me.
(22) I jumped into the chariot which was standing by the arena.

into those of

(23) The unicorn in the garden bothered me.
(24) I jumped into the chariot standing by the arena.

The RELATIVE CLAUSE REDUCTION Transformation, deleting the relative pronoun and the copula, is an important one. Stylistically its application produces more compact, after more elegant sentences — and, interestingly enough, not only in English. The Italian and French sentences and their English translations

(25) La cappelletta *che era* vecchia, scrostata, malandata, era a pochi passi.
(26) The shrine, *which was* old, peeling, dilapidated, was a few steps away.
(27) La boîte contenait des morceaux de paille *qui étaient* tordus et tressés en forme de cigarillos.
(28) The box contained bits of straw *which were* twisted and braided into the shape of cigarillos.

all have paraphrases to which RELATIVE CLAUSE REDUCTION has been applied:

(29) La cappelletta, vecchia, scrostata, malandata, era a pochi passi.
(30) The shrine, old, peeling, dilapidated, was a few steps away.
(31) La boîte contenait des morceaux de paille tordus et tressés en forme de cigarillos.
(32) The box contained bits of straw twisted and braided into the shape of cigarillos.

Relative clause reduction is also basic to the process by which adjectives are shifted in English to the left of the nouns they modify. Thus in French

---

[1] Note that there is a related transformation which actually deletes relative pronouns. The RELATIVE PRONOUN DELETION Transformation does delete relative pronouns but *only* when they are not subject noun phrases, for example, *The girl who Perseus rescued was Andromeda* and *The girl Perseus rescued was Andromeda*.

(33) la tête qui était ratatinée . . .
(34) the head which was shrivelled . . .

becomes

(35) la tête ratatinée . . .
(36) * the head shrivelled . . .

However, in English, the adjective has to be shifted around the noun:

(37) the shrivelled head . . .

This ADJECTIVE Transformation is normally applicable only when RELATIVE CLAUSE REDUCTION has taken place and when the predicate contains a single adjective (or verb, for that matter). Thus the structures underlying

(38) The mermaid who was $\left\{ \begin{array}{l} \text{long-haired} \\ \text{by the pool} \\ \text{singing} \\ \text{standing by the waterfall} \end{array} \right\}$ smiled coyly at Aloysius Cubberley

are converted by RELATIVE CLAUSE REDUCTION into those of

(39) the mermaid $\left\{ \begin{array}{l} \text{* long-haired} \\ \text{by the pool} \\ \text{singing} \\ \text{standing by the waterfall} \end{array} \right\}$ smiled coyly at Aloysius Cubberley.

The ADJECTIVE Transformation, which must be applied for the adjective *long-haired* and the verb *singing*, cannot be used for the preposition phrase, or for all or part of the verb phrase *standing by the water:*

(40) The $\left\{ \begin{array}{l} \text{long-haired} \\ \text{* by the pool} \\ \text{singing} \\ \text{standing} \end{array} \right\}$ mermaid . . .

The three transformations, then,

1. RELATIVE CLAUSE Transformation
2. RELATIVE CLAUSE REDUCTION Transformation
3. ADJECTIVE Transformation

account for the fact that as a speaker of English you understand the semantic relationships between *the mermaid* and *singing* in

(41)   The mermaids were singing and they had long hair

to be present also in the very different surface structures

(42)   the mermaids who were singing . . .
(43)   the mermaids singing . . .
(44)   the singing mermaids . . .

All four surface structures have a common deep structure. That's why they mean the same.

Exercises for Chapter Twelve

1. Write a sentence containing a relative clause based upon each of the sentences below. In each case the relativized noun phrase in your sentence should be the one italicized.

   Example: Ted sold *ice cream.*

   (possible answer) The ice cream that Ted sold was awful.
   (a) Sergei broke a tooth on his *harmonica.*
   (b) The grocer found *the price of peas* had gone up.
   (c) I want him to try and remember to send me *two hot bagels.*
   (d) *A man* isn't likely to surrender his rights easily.
   (e) Things are often seen to be less complex after *a good night's sleep.*

2. When the RELATIVE CLAUSE Transformation applies, what syntactic element gets replaced by a relative pronoun. Give some justification for your answer. In other words, how do you know?

3. Explain the origin in English of such common structures as *the blue frog.* What is the deep structure of such phrases and what transformational processes apply to them

4. Describe some functions that relative clauses serve in English. How might the same functions be served if relative clauses did not exist in English?

BIBLIOGRAPHY

ANNEAR, SANDRA. "Relative Clauses and Conjunctions," *Working Papers in Linguistics,* Report Number 1. Ohio State University, 1967.

BACH, EMMON. "Nouns and Noun Phrases," in Bach and Harms (eds.). *Universals in Linguistic Theory.* New York: Holt, 1967.

KURODA, SIGE-YUKI. "English Relativization and Certain Related Problems," *Language* 44 (1968), pp. 244–266.

Non-Restrictive Relatives and Stylistic Focus

13

Restrictive clauses are subordinate in meaning to the clause containing the antecedent; continuative clauses are more independent: Their contents may often be expressed by an independent statement . . .

It may also be pointed out that a sentence with a restrictive clause contains a single statement, one with a continuative clause contains two statements.

R. W. Zandvoort (1966)

Grammarians have long been aware of the synonymy of such pairs of sentences as the following:

(1) The mermaids had long hair and the mermaids were singing.
(2) The mermaids, who were singing, had long hair.

The clause, *who were singing,* is a non-restrictive relative clause and plays a very different semantic function from the same clause *restrictive* relative clause in

(3) The mermaids who were singing had long hair.

The restrictive sentence, the one without the commas, is concerned only with the class of *singing mermaids*, a subclass of all possible mermaids. In other words there may have been silent mermaids present as well. But the non-restrictive version is concerned with *all* the mermaids present rather than a restricted set of singing ones. The non-restrictive clause sentence implies that all the mermaids there were singing and all the mermaids had long hair. The non-restrictive relative clause appears to be equivalent to a conjunction of two sentences. Non-restrictive clauses could be generated, it is thought, from conjoined sentences via a special NON-RESTRICTIVE

CLAUSE Transformation which would operate upon the structure underlying

(4) The mermaids had long hair and the mermaids were singing.

Unlike the CONJUNCTION REDUCTION Transformation, the NON-RESTRICTIVE CLAUSE Transformation requires the noun phrases to be identical. Since the true conjoined sentences above have identical noun phrases, the second could be shifted to the position immediately after the first noun phrase:

(5) The mermaids, and the mermaids were singing, had long hair.

This parenthetic insertion would be grammatical itself if the second *the mermaids* were to be pronominalized.

(6) The mermaids, and they were singing, had long hair.

Alternatively the second identical noun phrase could be relativized and the conjunction "and" removed:

(7) The mermaids, who were singing, had long hair.

Deriving non-restrictive relative clauses from deep structures containing conjoined sentences captures rather convincingly the parenthetical qualities which both kinds of sentences share but which restrictive relatives lack. And the slight differences in interpretation between

(7) The mermaids, who were singing, had long hair.

and

(8) The mermaids, who had long hair, were singing.

is represented in the deep structure simply by the different ordering for the conjoined sentences, for example, for (1)

(4) The mermaids had long hair and the mermaids were singing.

and for (2)

(9) The mermaids were singing and the mermaids had long hair.

However neither the precise form of NON-RESTRICTIVE CLAUSE Transformation nor its relation to the restrictive clause rule is yet clear. For example, it is not known whether the non-restrictive clause is embedded in a noun phrase, as is the restrictive clause, or rather follows the noun phrase, as the pronunciation and punctuation suggests. Furthermore, there have been some linguists who have even suggested that *all* relative sentences are derived from conjoined sentences.

These conjectures serve to point up the relative uncertainty with which linguists view particular claims about deep structures, surface structures, and transformations. Still, it is clear that conjoined sentences form the basis of many of the most common syntactic structures in English. CONJUNCTION REDUCTION offers an explanation of the synonymy between conjoined sentences and reduced sentences. Similarly, the theory which says that non-restrictive relative clauses originate as conjoined sentences also provides an explanation of a synonymy recognized by all speakers of English. Thus, for present purposes, there is little reason not to accept these formulations as true for the phenomena they explain.

The RELATIVE CLAUSE REDUCTION Transformation described in Chapter Twelve also works for non-restrictive relative clauses and is quite commonly used for stylistic effect. This transformation, remember, converted

(10) The unicorn which was in the garden bothered me

into

(11) The unicorn in the garden bothered me.

The deletion of the relative pronoun and the copula (*be*) makes for a more compact immediate effect. But this transformation is used even more commonly with non-restrictive relatives, for example,

(12) Silas, who was an impetuous old man, raised his stick threateningly

which can be converted into

(13) Silas, an impetuous old man, raised his stick threateningly.

Sometimes this choice does not seem to be available. The following is an example:

(14) The small tables which someone purchased cheaply from a cafeteria shone garishly in the sun.

Since the relative clause does not contain the copula *be*, relative clause reduction cannot occur. But, if a copula can be introduced into the relative, then relative clause reduction is possible. The easiest way to do this is to convert the relative clause sentence into its passive equivalent. This yields

(15)   The small tables which were purchased cheaply (by someone) from a cafeteria shone garishly in the sun.

The *by someone* phrase is deletable by the regular transformation deleting indefinite elements from sentences. Now, since there is a copula *were*, RELATIVE CLAUSE REDUCTION can be used:

(16)   The small tables, purchased cheaply from a cafeteria, shone garishly in the sun.

The following passage has no examples of this combination of the PASSIVE and RELATIVE CLAUSE REDUCTION Transformations:

> They ate in groups of four at small square tables of synthetic marble which someone had purchased cheaply from a cafeteria that was discarding them. The rain which was falling across the high windows, which were high from the floor, had the effect of sealing in light and noise . . . Hook made haste to be among the first to enter their common sitting room, Andrews's old livingroom, which someone had furnished in black leather and equipped with a vast cold fireplace.

But it is difficult to assess the effect of applying these transformations to the passage above, which is a paraphrase of one written by John Updike. Here is the original, which makes more use of these transformations:

> They ate in groups of four at small square tables of synthetic marble purchased cheaply from a cafeteria that was discarding them. The rain falling across the high windows, high from the floor, had the effect of sealing in light and noise . . . Hook made haste to be amongst the first to enter their common sitting room, Andrews's old livingroom, furnished in black leather and equipped with a vast cold fireplace.

John Updike, *The Poorhouse Fair*

In Updike's version there is a very careful suppression of any mention of individual human beings who are not inmates, and a de-emphasis on actions that must have been by individual human beings. The old people are outcasts acted upon by anonymous institutional entities. One individual touch — an obvious intervention by the author — throws into focus, through its conversational idiom, the anonymous inhumanity which seeks to dehumanize the old people.

In the first version, for example, the relative clause contains a mention of a "someone" who had made an economical purchase:

(17)   . . . which someone had purchased cheaply from . . .

a clause derived from the structure underlying

(18)   someone had purchased cheaply small square tables of synthetic marble. . . .

If this is passivized:

(19)   small square tables of synthetic marble had been purchased cheaply by someone . . .

the agent noun phrase can be deleted

(20)   small square tables of synthetic marble had been purchased cheaply.

Since the subject noun phrase is identical to the one immediately preceding it in the higher sentence, this lower sentence can be relativized as

(21)   which had been purchased cheaply.

The effect of the passive, which shifted the agent phrase from the subject position, is to remove some of the focus of this clause from this unspecified person to the cheap tables at which the groups were sitting. The focus is less on what someone once did about the tables and more on the actual tables. The further deletion of the agent phrase subordinates still more the earlier purchasing event. The event has no stated human agency. One further step is possible — reducing the relative clause to a participial phrase. Thus

(22)   . . . which had been purchased cheaply . . .

becomes just

(23)   . . .purchased cheaply . . .

so that the purchase is made to seem of very little importance. On the other hand, the failure to transform

(24)   a cafeteria that was discarding them

into

(25)   a cafeteria discarding them

serves to emphasize the *discarding*. These tables, in a home for poor old people, were like the people who used them, unwanted and discarded as useless. The atmosphere is institutional. Only institutions, not people, are mentioned. The "someone" who might have infiltrated into the passage as a thrifty buyer was suppressed by the PASSIVE and AGENT DELETION Transformations. Even the purchasing act is reduced in importance except as a way of introducing another impersonal institution, a cafeteria, one which uses shoddy little fake marble tables. The same processes are used to eliminate any mention of an outside human being who must have arranged the furnishing of the sitting room. The clause

(26)   which someone had furnished in black leather

is reduced by the same set of transformations: PASSIVE, AGENT DELETION, and RELATIVE CLAUSE REDUCTION to

(27)   furnished in black leather

One other straightforward case of RELATIVE CLAUSE REDUCTION is seen in the conversion of

(28)   . . . rain which was falling across . . .

into

(29)   . . . rain falling across . . .

seems to be both a matter of euphony and focus. The focus is primarily on the causative relation between the falling rain and its "sealing-in" effect. The falling of the rain, expressed in its reduced syntactic phrase, is less of an assertion and more of a descriptive detail.

However, one other difference between the two passages is not so easily described. It is far from obvious that the phrase

(30)   the high windows, high from the floor . . .

is derived from the structure underlying

(31)   the windows, which were high from the floor

because the second *high* is a qualification of the first *high* rather than the *windows*. The reduced clause, if we accept the reduction analysis, is what was earlier a non-restrictive relative clause, related earlier still to something like

> (32)   the high windows — and by "high" I mean "high from the floor"

The final reduced version still retains the very human interpolated remark feeling about it, although no human speaker appears in the surface form. It's almost as if someone were saying, "I want you to understand just how it was.'" Of course the height of the windows from the floor would prevent the old people from being able to look outside while they ate. The inmates are thus very much shut off from the world outside. It's hardly surprising later in the book that when the outside world impinges on them briefly both the inmates and the outsiders are momentarily terrified.

The transformations discussed — EXTRAPOSITION, IT DELETION, PASSIVIZATION, and RELATIVE CLAUSE REDUCTION — have had two major effects:

1. shifting thematically important constituents to syntactic positions which received focus

and

2. removing entirely or backgrounding thematically distracting elements

From your point of view as a writer, exploitation of such processes can be a useful way of revising and checking your own prose. Where you have, without realizing it, used such processes, try converting the sentences back and say the revised sentence aloud. Where you haven't used the processes, try them and see. But from the point of view of the critic, establishing the effect of a particular kind of sentence structure cannot properly be done without taking into consideration the many other elements that make up the novel or other literary work under consideration.

Exercise for Chapter Thirteen

In the novel *Herzog*, Saul Bellow makes considerable use of the same processes, the PASSIVE and RELATIVE CLAUSE REDUCTION rules, to convert what might otherwise appear as a busy, active scene into one where things just happen and human beings seem to have little control. The only human beings involved are Moses Herzog and some workmen demolishing Herzog's own house. The only verbs going with Moses are *heard* and *felt*, which are really almost passive in meaning. Indeed they could very roughly be paraphrased as *came to the ears of* and *warmed* in the paragraph to be quoted. The workmen are mentioned in only one sentence and the rest of the passage concerns what inanimate objects do — they feed fire, pull air towards them, burn *gracefully* and quiver, all in a rather helpless and desultory way. Where transitive verbs are used, the passive form is almost inevitably chosen. What, if anything, happens if some of the transformations are not used in the way Bellow used them?

Try comparing and discussing these two passages. The second one is the paragraph that Bellow wrote.

> The afternoon was ending, and in the widening area of demolition the wreckage was feeding a fire. Moses heard the air as the flames softly pulled it towards them. He felt the heat. The workmen, who were heaping wood on the bonfire, threw strips of molding like javelins, and paint and varnish smoked like incense. The old flooring burned gracefully — the funeral of exhausted objects. Scaffolds which were walled with pink, white, green doors quivered as the six-wheeled trucks carried off fallen brick. A dazzling broth of atmospheric gases surrounded the sun, which was now leaving for New Jersey and the west.

> The afternoon was ending, and in the widening area of demolition was a fire, fed by the wreckage. Moses heard the air, softly pulled toward the flames, felt the heat. The workmen, heaping the bonfire with wood, threw strips of molding like javelins. Paint and varnish smoked like incense. The old flooring burned gracefully — the funeral of exhausted objects. Scaffolds walled with pink, white, green doors quivered as the six-wheeled trucks carried off fallen brick. The sun, now leaving for New Jersey and the west, was surrounded by a dazzling broth of atmospheric gases.

Saul Bellow, *Herzog*

BIBLIOGRAPHY

HIGGINSON, F. H. *Anna Livia Plurabelle: The Making of a Chapter.* Minneapolis: University of Minnesota Press, 1960.

HILDICK, WALLACE. *Word for Word, A Study of Authors' Alterations.* London: Faber, 1965.

Noun Phrase Complementation

14

As you have seen, the relative pronouns *who, which,* and *that* are
introduced into sentences by means of the RELATIVE CLAUSE
Transformation described in Chapter Twelve. The relative clauses
may introduce form, together with the preceding noun (and article,
if any), a noun phrase. Relativization is one way of embedding
sentence structures into noun phrases. The sentence

(1) I learned those things which would impress an examiner.

is thus derived from a structure something like this:

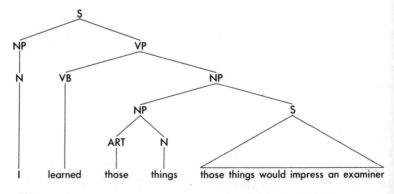

The second occurrence of *those things* is eventually replaced by *that* (or *which*). Note that the relative pronoun *that,* like the underlying *those things,* has an important grammatical role within the lower sentence. In this case is serves as subject.

There is another very important kind of embedding within a noun phrase that sometimes looks very much like relativization but which in reality is very different. The first *that* in the following passage is the ordinary relative pronoun. It serves in this case as subject of the relative clause. The relative pronoun *which* could serve in its place. But what about the second *that?*

(2)   Your job was to learn exactly those things *that* would give an examiner the impression *that* you knew more than you did know.

> George Orwell, "Such, Such Were the Joys . . ."

The second *that* cannot be replaced by *which.* Try it. Furthermore, in this case the embedded sentence could stand on its own as a sentence if the *that* were deleted. In other words, the word has no semantic interpretation whatever. It is not traceable back to a deep structure noun identical with the preceding noun *impression.* Yet the whole unit beginning with *the impression* is indeed a noun phrase, the direct object of the verb phrase. One common way of showing this is as follows:

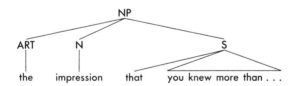

The semantic role of the embedded sentence in such is to provide detailed definition about the content of the abstract noun *impression.* In fact, the only nouns occurring in such structures are abstract nouns such as *fact, news, stories,* for example,

(3)   The fact that whales are mammals . . .
(4)   News that Alcindor was marching toward them . . .
(5)   Stories that the Bubonic Plague had attacked Florence . . .

Such embedded sentences are commonly said to function as *noun phrase complements* and the introducing element *that* is known as a *complementizer.* Tree diagrams may be used to differentiate relative clauses from noun phrase complements in the following fashion:

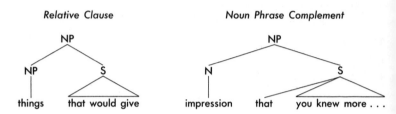

The relative pronoun is shown as grammatically involved in the relative clause. The complementizer, while forming a sentence structure with the complement, is more separate; and the complement sentence is shown as forming a sentence structure even without the complementizer *that.* (Diagrams are rather arbitrary ways of representing grammatical distinctions.)

Instead of an abstract noun preceding noun phrase complements, a rather special pronoun *it* may occur.

   (6)   Cardinal Heenan will see to *it that* the Cathedral is cleared.
   (7)   I dislike *it that you* change the regulations without notice.

This *it* is not the regular pronoun *it,* which must refer to a specific non-human thing. This *it* refers not to a single object but to the meaning of the whole complement sentence, just as the abstract nouns *impression, fact,* and *stories* did. However *it* rarely appears directly before its complement sentence. Almost always *it* is deleted. Thus sentence (6) above may be written

   (8)   Cardinal Heenan will see that the Cathedral is cleared.

without affecting the semantic interpretation. The preposition before *it* is also removed.

The complementizer *that* occurs without an abstract noun or *it,* as in

   (9)   That Sebastian was her brother was obvious to Viola.
   (10) That Aino wouldn't marry the old man surprised her mother.

The embedded sentences beginning sentences (9) and (10) are noun phrase complements without the expected noun preceding them. Indeed they are very much like the corresponding sentences below:

(11)   The fact that Sebastian was her brother was obvious to Viola.
(12)   The fact that Aino wouldn't marry the old man surprised her mother.

The difference is easily accounted for by suggesting that an *it* originally preceded the complement sentence and was deleted by the same IT DELETION Transformation which converted

Cardinal Heenan will see to it that . . .

into

Cardinal Heenan will see that . . .

Thus underlying sentences (9) and (10) are the following structures:

(13)   * it that Sebastian was her brother was obvious to Viola
(14)   * it that Aino wouldn't marry the old man surprised her mother

The IT DELETION Transformation normally deletes the *it* whenever *it* occurs immediately before a complement sentence. Except for a few special cases, this transformation is obligatory.

The transformation, EXTRAPOSITION, shifts embedded sentences from the position after "it" to the end of the sentence containing this pronoun. If the EXTRAPOSITION Transformation were applied to (13) and (14), the following sentences would be generated:

(15)   It was obvious to Viola that Sebastian was her brother.
(16)   It surprised her mother that Aino wouldn't marry the old man.

The EXTRAPOSITION Transformation is optional whereas the IT DELETION Transformation is obligatory. Since the *it* must be in the sentence for extraposition to be applied, the transformations are assumed to occur only in this order:

1. EXTRAPOSITION (optional)
2. IT DELETION (obligatory)

If the EXTRAPOSITION rule doesn't shift the embedded sentence, with the complementizer *that*, to the end of the higher sentence, then the *it* must be deleted by the second rule.

But now look at this pair of sentences:

(17) For the Moon King to have killed a mockingbird horrified the whole tribe.

(18) It horrified the whole tribe for the Moon King to have killed a mockingbird.

They seem to be related to each other in the same way that the following pair are related:

(19) That the Moon King had killed a mockingbird horrified the whole tribe.

(20) It horrified the whole tribe that the Moon King had killed a mockingbird.

Since sentences like (19) and (20) are related to a deeper structure:

(21) * it that the Moon King had killed a mockingbird horrified the whole tribe

it seems only reasonable to relate (17) and (18) to

(22) * it *for* the Moon King *to* have killed a mockingbird horrified the whole tribe

This could be shown this way in a tree diagram:

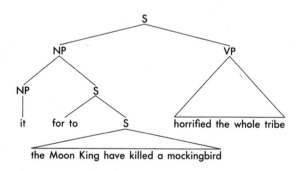

The words *for . . . to* constitute a complementizer in the same way as *that.* The *to* is transformationally moved to the position after the subject of the complement sentence, thus converting the verb into the infinitive form *to have killed.* The complementizer *for . . . to* is known as the *Infinitive Complementizer,* whereas *that* is called the *Clause Complementizer.*

There is, in fact, one other complementizer, the *Gerundive Complementizer,* which is observable in the sentence

(23) The Moon King's hav*ing* killed a mockingbird horrified the
      whole tribe.

The Gerundive Complementizer is thus the *POSSESSIVE . . . ing*.
The subject noun phrase becomes possessive, and *ing* is added to
the auxiliary or verb following after the subject noun phrase.

The three complementizers then are the

1. Clause Complementizer: *that*
2. Infinitive Complementizer: *for . . . to*
3. Gerundive Complementizer: *POSS . . . ing*

The Gerundive Complementizer differs from the others in generally
not allowing extraposition to be applied. IT DELETION must therefore always be used. There is, however, in some dialects of English,
a form which a complement sentence containing a gerundive complementizer appears to be extraposed:

(24) It horrified the whole tribe, the Moon King's having killed
      a mockingbird.

This sentence requires a comma in its written form and a pause (after
tribe) in its spoken form. Even so, for many speakers of English
this form is only marginally acceptable.

Certain subsidiary transformations are important in connection
with noun phrase complement constructions containing infinitive and
gerundive complementizers. The first, IDENTICAL NOUN PHRASE
DELETION, converts structures such as

(25) Kako preferred for Kako to drive the snakes away

and

(26) Scarlett O'Hara wanted for Scarlett O'Hara to marry Brett

into

(27) Kako preferred for to drive the snakes away

and

(28) Scarlett O'Hara wanted for to marry Brett.

In older forms of English, the first part of the complementizer,
for, could have remained. The following lines of fourteenth-century
English show the *for* part of the infinitive complementizer deleted
in the first line but retained in the second:

(29)   Thanne longen folk *to* goon on pilgrimages,
       And palmers *for to* seken straunge strondes . . .

       (Chaucer: General Prologue to *The Canterbury Tales*)

       (Then long folk to go on pilgrimages,
       And pilgrims to seek strange shores . . .)

In modern English, the deletion of *for,* known as COMPLE-MENTIZER DELETION is obligatory when it occurs before *to.*

Much the same process deletes the possessive part of the gerundive complementizer, converting

(30)   I dislike Marlowe's leaving us so soon

into

(31)   I dislike Marlowe leaving us so soon.

Similarly the complementizer *that,* converting

(32)   The Secretary-General reported that Lumumba had dis-appeared

into

(33)   The Secretary-General reported Lumumba had disappeared.

Not all complementizers are possible after many verbs. After *visualize,* for example, only the gerundive complementizer may be used:

(34)   * He visualized himself going.
(35)   * He visualized himself to go.
(36)   * He visualized that he went.

Even when verbs allow more than one complementizer, the meaning often varies. The grammarian Jespersen commented that "The infinitive seems more appropriate than the gerund to denote the imaginative (unreal), especially in the perfect."[1] Indeed some kind of presupposition is relevant here. After verbs like *see, detest,* and *understand,* complements are usually presupposed to have occurred. The Gerundive Complementizer is the one used:

[1] *A Modern English Grammar on Historical Principles, Part V,* London: George Allen and Unwin, 1961, Section 11.1.7

(37) I saw him coming and hid behind a palm tree.
(38) She detested his flattering her so often.
(39) They understood our resigning but disapproved.

Even verbs like *imagine* and *visualize* presuppose the event to occur, though not always in the real world.

On the other hand, *hope, expect,* and *order* do not presuppose and the infinitive complementizer is used

(40) They hope to arrive on Tuesday.
(41) We expect him to be in Quito tomorrow.
(42) Smirnov ordered him to eat the cactus.[2]

This all suggests that the analysis given in the first part of this chapter, though useful as a unifying hypothesis, is incomplete. It fails to account for important semantic distinctions: distinctions which should be treated as part of the basic meaning rather than the surface meaning arising from a particular stylistic configuration. A more adequate account of noun phrase complementation should allow the prediction on semantic grounds of one of the complement constructions rather than another. At present such an analysis does not exist. It awaits a more precise general formulation of the ways in which form is related to meaning in language. The Kiparsky and Kiparsky "Fact" paper referred to in the bibliography for this chapter represents a very interesting and useful attempt to deal with the problems of noun phrase complementation.

There is, however, a different perspective that is more closely related to the question of stylistic effect. Certain kinds of syntactic construction are easier to read and understand than other kinds.

It was pointed out in an earlier chapter that extraposition generally improves the readability of a sentence. And IT DELETION sometimes has the opposite effect. So

(43) That that is true is unfortunate

though grammatical, is best written

(44) It is unfortunate that that is true.

The grammatical complexity has now been shifted to the predicate part of the sentence. For some not well understood reason complexity

---

[2] For a useful discussion, see D. Bolinger's "Entailment and the Meaning of Structures" in *Glossa*, 2: 2 (1968) pp. 119–127.

on the right of a sentence is more easily understood than complexity on the left. Thus this passage is very difficult:

(45)   This house in which the malt that the rat that the cat killed ate lay was built by Jack.

If you read it very carefully and slowly, you will see that it means the same as:

(46)   This is the cat that killed the rat that ate the malt that lay in the house that Jack built

which is vastly more digestible.

Since EXTRAPOSITION shifts complexity to the right, it normally improves comprehensibility. Even when the IT DELETION sentence *is* understandable, the extraposed version may sound more balanced and rhythmic. From the sentence structure underlying

(47)   it that change is sometimes bad is true

you can get by IT DELETION:

(48)   That change is sometimes bad is true.

But this sentence with its big subject noun phrase and tiny predicate sounds a little topheavy (or, more accurately, "left-heavy"). The extraposed sentence sounds better; weight on the right sounds lighter than the same weight on the left:

(49)   It is true that change is sometimes bad.

In *Hamlet,* when Shakespeare makes fun of old Polonius, he has Polonius use complement sentences without EXTRAPOSITION:

(50)   My liege and madam, to expostulate
        What majesty should be, what duty is
        Why day is day, night night, and time is time
        Were nothing but to waste night, day, and time.

Hamlet, II ii 86–89

or one in which the extraposed complement is brought back to the left-hand side of the sentence:

(51)   That he's mad, 'tis true; 'tis true, 'tis pity . . .

Hamlet, II, ii, 97

Note that *that* must have been deleted from the beginning of the second part of the sentence:

(52)   That he's mad, 'tis true; that 'tis true, 'tis pity . . .

EXTRAPOSITION makes the sentence clearer:

(53)   It is true that he's mad; it is a pity that it is true . . .

However, when the right-hand side of a sentence is already too heavy, IT DELETION is preferable to EXTRAPOSITION. Thus

(54)   That change is sometimes bad is a truism too often used by those who oppose any kind of change at all no matter how bad the situation might be.

sounds a little less awkward than the extraposed paraphrase

(55)   It is a truism too often used by those who oppose any kind of change at all no matter how bad the situation might be that change is sometimes bad.

One problem with noun phrase complementation, nominalization, and any other process embedding one sentence structure inside another, is that, as in this sentence which you are presently reading, it is all too easy, even with a firm determination to express important ideas, to get lost inside a complex sentence and either to say things you don't mean or to make grammatical errors which won't seem obvious upon first reading but which impedes[3] comprehension. This type of problem is most commonly found in the writing of able high school or college students and in the correspondence columns of the more prestigious newspapers and periodicals.

First read the following outline of two arguments, which were probably used by an editor of the *Los Angeles Times*, N. B. Williams. Then see how a reader's letter arranges it so that a mass of noun phrase complements, nominalizations, and personification falls upon the argument like soft snow, blurring the outlines and covering up all the details.[4]

Here is the first argument:

1. In controversial matters people often take up extreme positions.
2. Once these positions are taken, people are apt to reject or ignore facts which do not support their positions.

----
[3] The error is deliberate!
[4] We are indebted to George Orwell for some of this sentence.

3. Thus they no longer seek truth. Instead they seek facts only to bolster up their opinions.
4. Therefore opinions should be treated as very tentative conclusions, which must be modified or rejected if more facts make this necessary. This preserves objectivity.

The second argument is brief:

5. Change is not always good but it is inevitable.
6. People who recognize the results of change do not necessarily either approve of them or advocate more of the same kinds of change.

Now here are three long sentences from a letter published in the *Los Angeles Times* on June 14, 1969:

(56)   The polarization of opinion is an enemy to the seeking of the truth and Williams did not in any way suggest that people give up their opinions but rather have them in a way that makes them susceptible to objectivity so necessary to growth and development.

To say that change is sometimes bad is true, and yet change we do, biologically, historically, politically and otherwise. To take the position that the recognition of the conditions created by change is to advocate them is a lie.

Just a few comments will be made here. The rest you should think about. The first part of the gigantic first sentence contains two nominalizations:

(57)   the polarization of opinion
(58)   the seeking of the truth

The subjects of the verbs in the underlying structure (*polarize, seek*) must have been indefinite noun phrases like *one* or *someone*. With the subjects removed, the noun phrases have become rather vague abstractions which must be handled very carefully. However the writer makes matters worse by personifying them. One nominalization is "an enemy" to the other. Later in the sentence she loses track and commits a grammatical sin. The verb *have* does not take adverbs of manner. You can say

(59)   Peter has a peck of pickled peppers.

but not

(60)   Peter has a peck of pickled peppers $\begin{Bmatrix} \text{promptly} \\ \text{pugnaciously} \\ \text{pensively} \\ \text{perseveringly} \end{Bmatrix}$

You can say *have an opinion* but not *have an opinion in a reasonable way* or

(61)   * Stokoe has an opinion in a way that sickens me

even though you can understand it. The writer produces exactly this anomaly:

(62)   have them in a way that . . .

and then embeds a whole series of nominalizations inside the *way* phrase.

The second sentence begins with an infinitive complement.

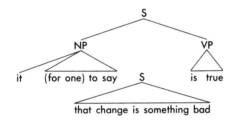

EXTRAPOSITION rather than IT DELETION makes the problem clearer:

(63)   It is true to say that change is sometimes bad.

Obviously the act of *saying* is not what is true. Truth is presumably claimed for the lowest sentence:

(64)   that change is sometimes bad.

If the *say* part is removed, the result is the more clear statement,

(65)   That change is sometimes bad is true

or, since the sentence is a little too heavy on the left, the extraposed version:

(66)   It is true that change is sometimes bad.

The same problem is even more obvious in the third sentence of (56), where *to take the position . . . is a lie.* The actual position may indeed include a lie, but *taking* a position is an action and an action can hardly be either a truth or a lie. Finally, within the position complement the writer connects a nominalized sentence with an infinitive complement using the copula *is:*

   (67) the recognition of the conditions created by change is to advocate them.

For some reason, embedded sentences on both sides of a copula must normally be of the same kind:

   (68) to recognize . . . is to advocate
   (69) recognition . . . is advocacy.

The funny thing is that if the writer had seen just the part of the sentence from *the recognition* to *advocate them,* she would probably have recognized the clumsiness. As it was, she was floundering in a syntactic morass.

Exercises for Chapter Fourteen

1. In your own words, describe some semantic differences between relative clauses and noun phrase complements.
2. Describe the essential syntactic differences between relative clauses and noun phrase complements, making explicit reference to how these structures are affected by transformational rules.
3. Draw deep structure diagrams for each of the following sentences:
   (a) The fellow wants a hearty meal.
   (b) The fellow wants to eat.
   (c) It annoys the clerk to work late.
4. List the transformations which generate the sentences in (3) from the deep structures you have created.
5. Construct four distinct sentences each of which illustrates the three creative linguistic processes you have studied thus far.

BIBLIOGRAPHY

BOLINGER, DWIGHT. "Entailment and the Meaning of Structures," *Glossa, 2:* 2 (1968) pp. 119–127.
KIPARSKY, PAUL and CAROL KIPARSKY. "Fact," in Manfred Bierwisch and Heidolph (eds.). *Recent Advances in Linguistics.* S-Gravenhage: Mouton, 1971.
ROSENBAUM, PETER S. *The Grammar of English Predicate Complement Constructions.* Cambridge. Mass.: M.I.T. Press, 1967.

Pronouns and the Mysteries of Pronominalization

15

If I or she should chance to be
Involved in this affair,
He trusts to you to set them free,
Exactly as we were.

Lewis Carroll (1865)

In *A Common-School Grammar of the English Language* (1866) Simon Kerl explains personal pronouns very carefully:

> When objects are near to us, or already known by having been mentioned, we do not always use their names, but certain little words in stead of the names. If I say, "William promised Mary that William would lend Mary William's grammar, that Mary might study the grammar," you can easily see that the sentence is clumsy and disagreeable, because I have repeated the words *William, Mary,* and *grammar.* . . . The easiest way in which you can generally distinguish a pronoun from a noun is to consider whether the word denotes an object, without being itself the name of the object.

Pronouns are indeed funny little words. Kerl's description of personal pronouns is a reasonable one, though it omits important aspects of the behavior of these words. Kerl improves his sentence by replacing the second instance of *William* with *he, Mary* with *she,* and so forth. But the pronoun *it* must replace not the noun *grammar* but the whole noun phrase *the grammar.* In fact *it* could be used to replace a long noun phrase like

(1)   . . . the musty-smelling grammar which William had purchased from Foyle's. . . .

In deep structure, pronouns are treated as a special class of noun. The noun-ness of pronouns is shown by including the feature

$\langle + \text{noun} \rangle$ as well as $\langle + \text{pronoun} \rangle$ as one of the set of features used to represent pronouns in deep structures. Like most other nouns, pronouns may be singular or plural:

$$
\underset{\begin{bmatrix} \langle + \text{N} \rangle \\ \langle + \text{pronoun} \rangle \\ \langle + \text{singular} \rangle \end{bmatrix}}{I}
\quad
\underset{\begin{bmatrix} \langle + \text{N} \rangle \\ \langle + \text{pronoun} \rangle \\ \langle - \text{singular} \rangle \end{bmatrix}}{we}
\quad
\underset{\begin{bmatrix} \langle + \text{N} \rangle \\ \langle + \text{pronoun} \rangle \end{bmatrix}}{you}
\quad
\underset{\begin{bmatrix} \langle + \text{N} \rangle \\ \langle + \text{pronoun} \rangle \end{bmatrix}}{you}
$$

Since the old singular form *thou* is no longer used, there is no need to specify singular or plural for *you* since the same form is used for both. But *I* and *we* differ from *you, they, he,* and so on, in that they are normally used by the speaker of the sentence to refer to himself or herself. They are therefore called *first person pronouns.* And *you* normally refers to the person or persons spoken to. It is called the second person pronoun. The other personal pronouns *he, she, it,* and *they* are usually used for whatever is not either the speaker (or writer) or the person(s) spoken to. They are the third person pronouns. So personal pronouns are shown with the person features (first person is $\langle + \text{I} \rangle$, second is $\langle + \text{II} \rangle$ and third $\langle + \text{III} \rangle$). In addition *he* differs from *she* in gender. That is, *he* can only be substituted for nouns or noun phrases referring to males, usually human ones, for example, *Sherlock Holmes, the man with a limp,* and sometimes an animal, such as *the bull. She* is used where females are referred to, and *it* where the sex is unspecified. So *she* and *he* and *it* are shown this way:

$$
\underset{\begin{bmatrix} \langle + \text{N} \rangle \\ \langle + \text{pronoun} \rangle \\ \langle + \text{feminine} \rangle \\ \langle + \text{III} \rangle \\ \langle + \text{singular} \rangle \end{bmatrix}}{she}
\qquad
\underset{\begin{bmatrix} \langle + \text{N} \rangle \\ \langle + \text{pronoun} \rangle \\ \langle + \text{masculine} \rangle \\ \langle + \text{III} \rangle \\ \langle + \text{singular} \rangle \end{bmatrix}}{he}
\qquad
\underset{\begin{bmatrix} \langle + \text{N} \rangle \\ \langle + \text{pronoun} \rangle \\ \langle + \text{III} \rangle \\ \langle + \text{singular} \rangle \end{bmatrix}}{it}
$$

What about the forms *me, us, her, him,* and *them?* These forms are used in many positions but not usually in the subject position. Within the present grammatical framework, this can be represented as a change from non-accusative or non-objective to accusative or objective. It is assumed that all nouns start off as non-accusative $\langle - \text{accusative} \rangle$. They get changed to accusative $\langle + \text{accusative} \rangle$ when they occur as anything but the subject of a sentence or clause. The obvious name for this is the ACCUSATIVE Transformation. Note that this would work for *all* nouns. The reason is that when, for example, a pronoun is substituted for *Dr. Chase* in

(2)   The club denounced Dr. Chase.

it takes on not only the person $\langle + \text{III} \rangle$, number $\langle + \text{singular} \rangle$, and gender $\langle + \text{masculine} \rangle$, but also what is called the *case* feature, $\langle + \text{accusative} \rangle$. Thus only the first of these two sentences is correct:

(3)   The club denounced him.
(4)   * The club denounced he.

The noun phrase *Dr. Chase* must therefore have been $\langle + \text{accusative} \rangle$.

The ACCUSATIVE Transformation, as described here, will produce

(5)   It is me.

or the contracted form

(6)   It's me.

but will not allow the purist's

(7)   It is I.

Speakers of this dialect do not apply the accusative transformation where the verb of a clause or sentence is the copula verb *be*.

This is far from being the whole story about the properties of personal pronouns. For example, pronouns are often used in about the same way as articles, for example:

(8)   the mariners
       you mariners
       we Americans

The pronouns discussed above are always definite, like the articles *the, this,* and *that.* It is sometimes claimed that in surface structure pronouns are really articles. Moreover the person features (+ I, II, III) are more complex than the present description suggests. For example, *we* is sometimes used to refer to a group which includes people spoken to, $\langle + \text{II} \rangle$. Sometimes it excludes those spoken to. The difference between the two is seen in these two sentences:

(9)   *We* are going to give you ten seconds to come out of there
       with your hands up and your hair braided.
(10)   *We* are going to capture Jericho, aren't we?

The way that pronouns work in a language is indeed not too well understood. To say that they stand for nouns (or noun phrases) is not enough, since they are used in at least two different ways. Sometimes they are used in the way illustrated by Simon Kerl, to replace the second mention of the noun phrase. Thus

(11) Soames claimed Soames was related to Sir Winston Churchill.

is normally converted into

(12) Soames claimed he was related to Sir Winston Churchill.

But sometimes a personal pronoun represents not a noun phrase previously mentioned in the sentence but someone or something else. Thus the last example sentence is actually ambiguous. The pronoun *he* could also refer to someone other than *Soames*, possibly someone whose name was unknown. Pronominalization, the process of converting a noun phrase (like *Soames*) into a pronoun (*he*) thus could not be the whole story. Pronouns can occur in deep structures in the same way as nouns do:

(13) He removed the glass cover.

or they can result from the PRONOMINALIZATION Transformation converting a repeated noun phrase into the pronoun form by adding the feature $\langle +\text{pronoun} \rangle$. This dual source for pronouns accounts for the ambiguity.

But even here matters are hardly as simple as they seem. For example, assume that the underlined pronouns in the following sentences are all the result of the PRONOMINALIZATION Transformation. That is, where two noun phrases are italicized they refer to the same person. These sentences are quite acceptable:

(14) *Dr. Johnson* said that *he* hated Scotland.
(15) *Dr. Johnson* admired Pope but *he* despised Cowley.

But the following are not:

(16) *He* said that *Dr. Johnson* hated Scotland
(17) *He* admired Pope but *Dr. Johnson* despised Cowley

if *he* refers to Dr. Johnson. It seems that such pronominalization occurs in a left to right direction. It doesn't appear to matter how far away the pronoun form if from the noun phrase it refers to as long as the pronoun is to the right of the noun phrase:

(18)   *Dr. Johnson* disliked Lady Montague, only tolerated women who understood their subordinate role in society, and took delight in insulting women who were thought by *him* to be too forward.

(19)   * *He* disliked Lady Montague, only tolerated women who understood their subordinate role in society, and took delight in insulting women who were thought by *Dr. Johnson* to be too forward.

The pronoun *he* can only occur in the last example if it does not refer to Dr. Johnson.

But the assumption that pronominalization can *only* take place in a rightward direction must be rejected, as the following sentences suggest:

(20)   Although *he* attacked Cowley and other poets like him, *Dr. Johnson* was one of the few critics of the time who understood what these poets were trying to do.

(21)   From the moment that *he* entered the room *Dr. Johnson* dominated the conversation.

These and other examples suggest that pronominalization *can* go leftward if the form to be pronominalized is in a subordinate clause while the other noun phrase is in a higher clause.

So pronominalization is normally a rightward (or forward) direction, but it can operate leftward (or backward) where the noun phrase to be pronominalized is in a lower sentence structure than the other phrase having the same reference.

In fact there are cases which require that the conclusions above be further amended and made more precise. But what is especially interesting, however the grammarian explains the facts of pronouns, is that the conditions governing pronoun forms are very much like those governing deletion of identical noun phrases and also a number of grammatical processes involved in the formation of interrogative and negative sentences. Apparently there are some more general principles that are not properly understood at present. If these can be isolated, and if they turn out to be true for other languages, then linguists will be considerably closer to understanding the mystery that is language.

Exercises for Chapter Fifteen

1. Construct dictionary (feature composition) entries for the following pronouns:

   I, we, they (feminine), it, be, you (plural)

2. Draw tree diagrams for the two deep structures underlying the following ambiguous sentence:

   Jones mentioned the fact that he snores.

3. Describe as precisely as you can the exact circumstances under which pronouns acquire the feature ⟨+accusative⟩.

4. Why might one want to consider the hypothesis that pronouns are analyzable more properly as articles rather than real nouns in the surface structure?

5. Compare the sentences below:
   (a) Drop your gun or I'll shoot it out of your hand!
   (b) Drop it or I'll shoot your gun out of your hand!
   The *it* in the (a) sentence can refer to *your gun* but *it* in the (b) sentence cannot. What does this suggest about the workings of the PRONOMINALIZATION Transformation?

6. Now consider this sentence:

   If you don't drop it, I'll shoot your gun out of your hand.

   Here, *it* can refer to *your gun.* What assumptions would you have to make about the ordering of the PRONOMINALIZATION Transformation and the transformation (let's call it the IF CLAUSE Transformation) which moves the *if* clause from the back of the sentence to the front if you are going to seriously maintain the claims you made in Exercise 5?

BIBLIOGRAPHY

LANGACKER, RONALD. "Pronominalization and the Chain of Command," in David Reibel and Sanford Schane (eds.). *Modern Studies in English.* Englewood Cliffs, N. J.: Prentice-Hall, 1969.

McCAWLEY, JAMES. "Where Do Noun Phrases Come From?" in R.A. Jacobs and P.S. Rosenbaum (eds.). *Readings in English Transformational Grammar.* Waltham, Mass.: Ginn, 1970.

POSTAL, PAUL M. "On the So-Called Pronoun in English," in Jacobs and Rosenbaum, *Readings.*

Grammar and Explanation

16

In a word, what I am trying to say, what all my preliminary admonitions boil down to, is simply this: Language is
exceedingly complicated. Forgive me for taking so long
to say such a simple and obvious thing.

George A. Miller (1965)

As you have seen from your studies in this book, the English language
is far more complex than your old school grammar books suggested.
But its complexity is not arbitrary. English reveals a set of systematic
and regular processes. The type of language analysis presented in
this book, transformational analysis, is still in its infancy, and only
a few of the principles have been recognized. Sometimes it is obvious
that some important principle is governing particular sentence forms
and their interpretations, but exactly what the principle is still remains a mystery. A linguist investigating particular kinds of constructions must try not just to catalog and label, but also to explain.
The linguist's aim is to explain how native speakers of English
understand particular forms and to show why apparently like forms
are interpreted differently or why apparently different forms are
interpreted alike. He would also like to show that apparent irregularity is a part of an underlying regularity, to show how the fragment
of syntax he is describing is related to other aspects of English syntax.

In this chapter we would like to give you some feeling for the
kind of questions that research linguists interested in English grammar are currently investigating. For this purpose we have selected
the phenomenon of *negation* and our concern will be with an apparently arbitrary irregularity in the interpretation of certain negative
sentences. We will try to explain this irregularity by looking more
closely at its semantic interpretation and by deriving from it (1) a

suggestion about deep structure and (2) a particular transformation needed to convert the hypothesized underlying structure into the surface form. You will see that independent evidence exists to justify the analysis and that the analysis accounts for the properties described. But you will also see that there is yet a more general principle somehow involved, one that still evades analysis. It seems to be connected with the important and very puzzling matter of presupposition: information that is presupposed to be true by the speaker or writer of the sentence. Let us begin.

Negation is a major process for modifying the meaning of sentences in any language. If two sentences are identical except that one has a negative element and the other doesn't, the sentences should be quite differently interpreted. Thus the sentence

(1)   I remembered that Barclay left the bank

is understood differently from

(2)   I didn't remember that Barclay left the bank.

The latter sentence contains a negative in its main clause. The following tree shows the relevant information as to structure:

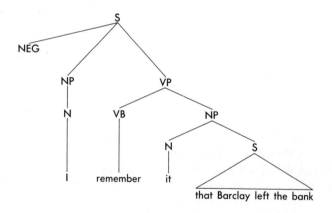

The upper sentence contains the negative element, which will later become *didn't*. The embedded sentence has no negative element.

But suppose the negative element was in the lower sentence instead:

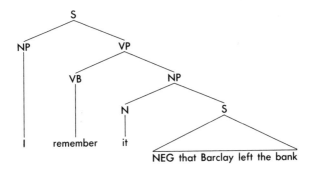

As you would suspect, the two sentences have quite distinct interpretations:

(2)   I didn't remember that Barclay left the bank.
(3)   I remembered that Barclay didn't leave the bank.

The second sentence tells of a definite act of remembering. The first could well be about forgetting. The semantic difference is represented by positioning the negative in the upper sentence in the first case, and in the lower sentence in the second case. The same kind of difference is to be seen in:

(4)   I wasn't aware that Barclay had left the bank.
(5)   I was aware that Barclay hadn't left the bank.

or

(6)   I didn't know that Barclay was a bank robber.
(7)   I knew that Barclay wasn't a bank robber.

and so on.

But there are some problem sentences that also need to be accounted for. For most people, these two sentences can be synonymous:

(8)   I thought that Barclay wasn't very clever.
(9)   I didn't think that Barclay was very clever.

and these:

(10)   I believed that Barclay hadn't left the bank yet.
(11)   I didn't believe that Barclay had left the bank yet.

and these:

(12)   It's likely that Barclay won't be captured until tomorrow.
(13)   It's not likely that Barclay will be captured until tomorrow.

In these cases, it doesn't seem to make any difference where the negative element occurs. In the other cases, which happen to be much more common, it did make a difference. How can this difference be explained?

You have already seen in earlier chapters that synonymous sentences are assumed to share a common deep structure. So

(14) I thought that Barclay wasn't very clever.

and

(15) I didn't think that Barclay was very clever.

must share a common structure with the negative in one, and only one, position. Otherwise the sentence would be:

(16) I didn't think that Barclay wasn't very clever.

The question is, where should the negative originate?

Since deep structure is supposed to represent meaning, what is the *meaning* of each clause? Is it implied in both sentences either that the speaker thought anything *or* that he didn't think anything? In fact, thinking is implied in *both* sentences. When you say something like *I didn't think that such and such* it implies thinking as much as saying something like *I thought that such and such.* The higher sentence, then, might be thought to start off without a negative element. What about the lower sentence? In either sentence, is it the speaker's opinion that Barclay really was clever, or that he wasn't? Clearly the speaker of either sentence has a negative view of Barclay's cleverness. Semantically, the negation is in the lower sentence. The deep structure is thus representable something like this:

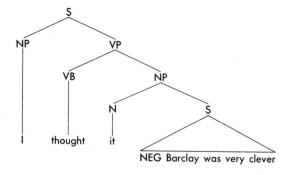

So some transformation, call it NEG RAISING, must raise the negative element from the lower sentence into the upper sentence. Since transformations themselves do not change meaning, the basic meaning would not be affected by the negating transformation. Of course this transformation works only if the verb or adjective in the upper sentence is one like *think, believe, likely;* not one like *remember, know,* or *aware.* (Note that this is one more case where verbs and adjectives are much alike.)

There are some interesting properties associated with these two groups of verbals. The sentences

(17) It is regrettable that Barclay left.
(18) I remembered that Barclay left.
(19) I was aware that Barclay left.
(20) It isn't regrettable that Barclay left.
(21) I didn't remember that Barclay left.
(22) I wasn't aware that Barclay left.

all are interpretable as *presupposing* that Barclay actually did leave. (There are additional interpretations but these are not important here.) On the other hand, it is clear that the speaker has no such definite *knowledge* in:

(23) I think that Barclay has left.
(24) I believe that Barclay has left.
(25) It is likely that Barclay has left.
(26) I don't think that Barclay has left.
(27) I don't believe that Barclay has left.
(28) It isn't likely that Barclay has left.

The speaker of these sentences accepts the possibility that he might be wrong. Thus he could later say

(29) I thought that Barclay had left, but I was wrong.

However, the verbals of presupposition leave no such possibility. Thus the following sentences are strange ones:

(30) I remembered that Barclay had left but I was wrong.
(31) It was regrettable that Barclay had left but in fact he hadn't.

So the difference with regard to NEGATIVE RAISING is also matched by other important differences, both semantic and syntactic. How these differences are related is presently unclear. But it is probably no coincidence that verbals which happen not to involve presupposition also allow NEGATIVE RAISING, while presupposition verbals do not. This correlation must have to do with some important ways of incorporating into language the speaker's views of reality.

The evidence so far presented for the existence of NEGATIVE RAISING has been entirely semantic in nature; for example, recourse to the fact of the synonymy of the *I don't think* and *I think* sentences. But the argument would be much more compelling if some syntactic evidence could be found for this transformation. If there truly is such a process in English syntax as NEGATIVE RAISING, evidence might be found in the actual forms of the sentences. Let's see. The claim made by the NEGATIVE RAISING hypothesis is that the lower sentence in, for example,

(32)   I didn't believe that Barclay had left the bank

that is, *Barclay had left the bank* must originally have contained a negative. The negative was later raised into the higher sentence.

There are certain words and groups of words which, it turns out, can occur only with negatives. They include *can help, until too late, yet, lift a finger, at all,* and *ever.*[1] (Most of these can also occur in interrogative sentences.) Thus you can say

(33)   Barclay can't help robbing banks.
(34)   Barclay didn't realize until too late that . . .
(35)   Barclay hadn't arrived yet.
(36)   Barclay didn't lift a finger to save her.

but not (with ordinary intonation)

(37)   Barclay can help robbing banks.
(38)   Barclay realized until too late that . . .
(39)   Barclay had arrived yet.
(40)   Barclay lifted a finger to save her.

This requirement for a negative extends to cases when the sentence is embedded in a lower one. Thus it is all right to say sentences like:

---

[1] Most of these can also occur in interrogative sentences, and there are, of course, sentences like "I can help you change that tire" and "It's the best concert ever" which are not relevant to the present discussion.

(41)   We remembered that Barclay can't help robbing banks.
(42)   We were aware that Barclay didn't realize until too late
       that . . .

but not sentences like:

(43)   We remembered that Barclay can help robbing banks.
(44)   We were aware that Barclay realized until too late that . . .

So whether in an independent sentence

(45)   * Barclay has left the bank yet

or embedded in another sentence

(46)   * We knew that Barclay had left the bank yet

the word *yet* apparently can exist only in a negative sentence.

Now here finally is some firm evidence that NEGATIVE RAISING is a real syntactic process in English. It is quite grammatical to use *yet* in

(47)   I didn't believe that Barclay had left the bank yet.

In fact all the other phrases that normally require negatives can occur after verbals like *believe, think*, and *likely*.

(48)   I don't think that Barclay can help robbing banks.
(49)   It isn't likely that Barclay lifted a finger to save her.
(50)   I don't believe that Barclay realized until too late that . . .

The presence of these *negative* phrases only with the verbs for which NEGATIVE RAISING is postulated provides some syntactic confirmation that the lower sentences containing the *negative* phrases must once have contained a negative, one which was later raised. Otherwise, the words like *yet* and *until too late* could not appear in the lower sentence without producing a semantically peculiar sentence.

The sentences were presumably:

(51)   I think that Barclay can't help robbing banks.
(52)   It is likely that Barclay didn't lift a finger to save her.
(53)   I believe that Barclay didn't realize until too late that . . .

So, the apparently irregular synonymy of sentences containing certain verbs, for example, *think*, can be accounted for by positing a NEGATIVE RAISING Transformation. This was first suggested on the basis of semantic criteria. But then the transformation was found to be necessary not only to explain the synonymy but also to account for the apparently irregular behavior of *yet, until too late, can help,* and *lift a finger* in just those sentences for which negative raising was suggested.

BIBLIOGRAPHY

KIPARSKY, PAUL and CAROL. "Fact," in Bierwisch and Heidolph (eds.). *Recent Advances in Linguistics.* S-Gravenhage: Mouton, 1971.
KLIMA, EDWARD. "Negation in English," in Fodor and Katz. *The Structure of Language.* Englewood Cliffs, N. J.: Prentice-Hall, 1964, pp. 246–323.

Of Words and Style and Syntax and Meaning and Everything

17

I feel that "terrible" is uncommunicated, fails of its meaning, and to a lesser extent that "bitter" does not work
.... Somehow the adjective weakens the noun speed. It
is not sufficiently motivated. . . .

> *Richard Eberhart on Richard Wilbur's*
> *poem "Love Calls us to the Things of*
> *This World"*

If the surprising words of a poem are also adjectives, they
seem (first-off, at least) like chromium accessories on a
jalopy, or flashy costume jewelry on a woman with a bad
figure. Nouns and verbs make the power and figure of a
poem.

Nevertheless, the general strategy and local syntax of a
poem will sometimes force one to put in an adjective
what might be stronger elsewhere . . . the love of line 23
has got to be bitter — for the sake of psychological truth.
Again I agree that the necessity would be plainer, at first
look, if the extrusive word were not an adjective. Had I
been able to afford another "speech" at that point in the
poem, I might have conveyed the notion of bitter love
dramatically. . . .

> *Richard Wilbur responding to*
> *Eberhart's criticism.*

The quotations heading this chapter reflect a concern with an area
of style and meaning that has received little attention here, since
this book has concentrated primarily on the contribution of *syntax*
to style and meaning. Yet concern for the range of meanings and
associations of particular word choices is necessarily an important
part of a full theory of style. The adjectives *terrible* and *bitter* in

the context of Wilbur's poem have, for Richard Eberhart, too wide a range of meanings, both basic and associational, and the structure of the poem fails to define the meanings more narrowly. In a sense, then, the poet is cheating — allowing these open-ended words to be restricted by the imagination and experience of the reader. The reader is thus doing work customarily regarded as the function of the poet. The comments both of Eberhart and Wilbur on adjectives are somewhat overstated. Verbs usually do have an "active" character and nouns a "thingness" quality that together seem to amount to the basic facts of human experience. And adjectives like *bitter, terrible, strange,* or *gloomy* serve a summarizing function of the effects of the phenomena so described upon a particular human awareness or perhaps a generalized human awareness. But generalizations about word classes are easily overstated.

As abbreviations, such adjectives *can* be replaced with an enumeration or dramatization of the actual qualities of the phenomena that led the poet to evaluate it as *bitter, terrible, strange,* or *gloomy.* As Wilbur points out, other considerations (*general strategy* . . .) determine the stylistic choices. But of course not all adjectives are abbreviatory devices in this sense. Words like *hungry, instinctive, grassy, reddish-brown* make statements of their own which cannot easily be replaced by dramatizations. They have a different orientation, one less focused on the individual consciousness of the experiencer and more upon the less subjective qualities of the phenomena experienced.

Although one of the major thrusts of modern literary criticism has been toward the study of the effects of particular word choices, little effort has been made in criticism to work out methodically the individual areas of meaning represented by crucial word choices. For example the experiencer–object orientation referred to in the previous paragraph is part of a wider orientation phenomenon that may be universal. In English the verbs *start, cease,* and *stop* are more often oriented toward the actor in a sentence, while *begin, finish,* and *complete* are oriented toward the object of the action. For example, in the sentences

(1) Stanley $\begin{Bmatrix} \text{ceased} \\ \text{stopped} \end{Bmatrix}$ painting the wall.

(2) Stanley finished painting the wall.

a point of time is assumed when Stanley is no longer painting the wall. But the second sentence indicates that there is no more wall requiring paint. The emphasis is on the condition of the wall. In the first sentence the emphasis is less on the wall and more on the cessation of action by Stanley. Since the orientation is towards Stanley rather than the wall, the verb *painting* cannot be removed — Stanley could do (or stop doing) innumerable things to the wall:

(3)   * Stanley $\begin{Bmatrix} \text{started} \\ \text{stopped} \\ \text{ceased} \end{Bmatrix}$ the wall.[1]

But in (2), where the wall is more the focus, the verb *painting* can be omitted since it is one of the culturally expected actions that may be performed to change the nature of a wall:

(4)   Stanley $\begin{Bmatrix} \text{began} \\ \text{finished} \end{Bmatrix}$ the wall.

In particular contexts (4) can be understood as meaning that Stanley was building, painting, demolishing (etc.) a wall, but not normally that he was looking at it, climbing it, kicking or licking it. Where the orientation is toward the object, the semantic field of possible unspecified verbs is fairly restricted. According to general transformational theory, such "deletions" must be recoverable, that is, we must be able to tell what has been omitted. Such examples suggest that the deep structure contains semantic rather than purely formal elements and that not all the elements need be fully specified at that level.

In a rather crude sense there is a lexical analogue to the notions of basic meaning and surface meaning described earlier in this book, especially in Chapter One. The basic meaning corresponds roughly to the dictionary meanings of the words, though dictionary entries lack the hierarchical structures and implicational facts needed to express the network of interdependencies and presuppositions that characterize meaning in natural languages. The surface meaning corresponds even more approximately to the associations a word takes on, for example, as a result of any sound-symbolisms, or as a member of a set of recurring thematically-significant elements.

Wilbur's talk of *conveying the notion of bitter love* seems at first to imply a form–content separation. He appears to be claiming that

---

[1] Note that in many dialects the sentence with *start* is acceptable. This verb, in these dialects, allows for object orientation.

notions can be clothed in a number of distinct forms without any effect on meaning. This is obviously incorrect even on the basis of the Eberhart–Wilbur discussions. But Wilbur's rather vague *general strategy and local syntax* qualifies this and shows his awareness of an important area of meaning controlled by the larger units of discourse chosen.

This is not to suggest any kind of isomorphic relationship between particular syntactic forms and, say, kinds of thematic content. But that there can be an important correlation between syntactic form and thematic content is undeniable. The opening of Chaucer's *Canterbury Tales* shows such a correlation:

> **Whan that Aprille with his shoures sote**
> **The droughte of Marche hath perced to the rote,**
> **And bathed every veyne in swich licour,**
> **Of which vertu engendred is the flour;**
> **Whan Zephirus eek with his swete breeth**
> **Inspired hath in every holt and heeth**
> **The tendre croppes, and the yonge sonne**
> **Hath in the Ram his halfe cours y-ronne,**
> **And smale fowles maken melodye,**
> **That slepen al the night with open yë,**
> **(So priketh hem nature in hir courages):**
> **Than longen folk to goon on pilgrimages . . .**

Chaucer is focusing on the coming of spring as a particular but recurrent point in time when life begins to reawaken. He does this in a series of *when* clauses whose subjects are the causers of the awakening: *Aprille, Zephirus* (the West Wind), *the yonge sonne* (sun). The long series of subordinate clauses climaxes in the highest (or main) clause, which both echoes and rounds off the earlier *when*'s with a resounding *then*. Corresponding fairly closely to this hierarchical syntactic structure is a hierarchical ordering of the natural elements which figure in this drama of awakening. The ordering goes from the natural elements — showers, wind and sun — to the vegetable world — flowers, and *tendre croppes* (shoots) — to *smale fowles,* and finally, in the main clause, to the *folk.* Significantly these *folk* long to go on *pilgrimages,* this last word suggesting a yet higher order, the divine one.

But although the order is an ascending one, the parallel structuring of the clauses, from the most embedded to the highest clause, emphasizes what all share. They all share this great upsurge of spring life.

Man's fidgety desire to go on pilgrimages, lofty as it might seem in isolation, is somewhat humorously related to the springtime restlessness of all life. All suffer from the great itch. Man is very much a harmonious part of this great chain of being. His position is a sure one — below God but above the animals, as the hierarchical ordering of the syntax implies.

This sense of stability with the hierarchy of life is all the more obvious when contrasted with the unease of the opening of the great April poem of this century, T. S. Eliot's *The Wasteland:*

> April is the cruellest month, breeding
> Lilacs out of the dead land, mixing
> Memory and desire, stirring
> Dull roots with spring rain.
> Winter kept us warm, covering
> Earth in forgetful snow, feeding
> A little life with dried tubers.
> Summer surprised us, coming over the Starnbergersee
> With a shower of rain; we stopped in the colonnade,
> And went on in sunlight, into the Hofgarten,
> And drank coffee, and talked for an hour.

Here man is no longer in harmony with nature, though ironically, he is more explicitly equated in the metaphoric structure: . . . *stirring dull roots . . . feeding . . . with dried tubers.* Spring and summer are neither expected nor desired. Far from being in harmony with the seasons, man is *surprised* by summer. And where, in Chaucer's poem, the new movement spurs man into affirmation through pilgrimage, here the activities are random, purposeless: stopping in the colonnade, drinking coffee, talking for an hour. Eliot's lines lack the tight hierarchical ordering of the earlier poem. Statements are made and then participial phrases expand on the statements, with none of the powerful forward movement of Chaucer's *Prologue.* The culminating activities are anticlimactic, trivial, and without purposeful ordering: *stopped . . . and went on . . . And drank coffee, and talked for an hour.* and the conjoining with *and*'s emphasizes the lack of hierarchical ordering. All this is not to suggest that Eliot's work is inferior. It is, in fact, a powerful expression of dissatisfaction with an aimless, rootless, and orderless world, a dissatisfaction arising from values not so different from those that Chaucer was able to take for granted.

But here an important question arises. The syntactic format of each passage is admirably in harmony with its thematic elements. Is a hierarchically-organized sentence form necessary to express in the most effective way the character of a hierarchically-ordered universe? And correspondingly are the superficially aimless syntactic forms in the Eliot passage necessary for such a poem? Obviously this cannot be properly answered without the evidence of thematically similar but syntactically different literary works. But even without this it should be obvious that the syntax does not *have to* reflect the thematic content in the ways described above.

The relation between form and meaning is thus a very complex one involving many other factors besides syntax and vocabulary. That syntax plays an important, even crucial role is suggested in our earlier analyses of prose by George Eliot, Updike, Baldwin, and Bellow. This book presents only a tentative map for future exploration. An accurate description of the syntactic forms and a more detailed formulation of their contribution to the overall impact of a literary work is a necessary preliminary for establishing an adequate theory of style and, more importantly, for understanding just how the forms of language mirror the forms of thought. As Leibniz wrote, "languages are the best mirror of the human mind."

BIBLIOGRAPHY

DIXON, ROBERT M. W. "A Method of Semantic Description, Illustrated for Dyirbal Verbs," in D. Steinberg and L. Jacobovits (eds.). *Semantics: An Interdisciplinary Reader.* Champaign: University of Illinois Press, 1971.

DIXON, ROBERT M. W. "Syntactic Orientation as a Semantic Property" in Report No. NSF-24. Cambridge, Mass.: The Computation Laboratory of Harvard University, 1970.

JAKOBSON, ROMAN. "On the Verbal Art of William Blake and Other Poet-Painters," in *Linguistic Inquiry, 1;* 1 (January 1970), pp. 3–25.

KUNO, SUSUMU. "Feature-Changing Rules in Semantics," in Report No. NSF-24, *op. cit.*

OSTROFF, ANTHONY (ed.). *The Contemporary Poet as Artist and Critic.* Boston: Little, Brown, 1964.

POSTAL, PAUL M. "On the Surface Verb 'Remind'," in *Linguistic Inquiry, 1;* 1 (January 1970), pp. 37–121.